B. Disraeli

Lothair by the Right Honorable B. Disraeli "Lothair" 2

B. Disraeli

Lothair by the Right Honorable B. Disraeli "Lothair" 2

ISBN/EAN: 9783741173424

Manufactured in Europe, USA, Canada, Australia, Japa

Cover: Foto ©Thomas Meinert / pixelio.de

Manufactured and distributed by brebook publishing software
(www.brebook.com)

B. Disraeli

Lothair by the Right Honorable B. Disraeli "Lothair" 2

COLLECTION

OF

BRITISH AUTHORS

TAUCHNITZ EDITION.

VOL. 1095.

LOTHAIR

BY

THE RIGHT HONORABLE B. DISRAELL

IN TWO VOLUMES.

VOL. II.

LOTHAIR.

BY THE

RIGHT HONORABLE B. DISRAELI.

COPYRIGHT EDITION.

IN TWO VOLUMES.

VOL. II.

LEIPZIG
BERNHARD TAUCHNITZ
1870.

LOTHAIR.

CHAPTER I.

On the morrow, the early celebration in the chapel was numerously attended. The Duchess and her daughters, Lady Agramont, and Mrs. Ardenne were among the faithful; but what encouraged and gratified the Bishop was, that the laymen, on whom he less relied, were numerously represented. The Lord Lieutenant, Lord Carisbrooke, Lord Montairy, Bertram, and Hugo Bohun accompanied Lothair to the altar.

After the celebration, Lothair retired to his private apartments. It was arranged that he was to join his assembled friends at noon, when he would receive their congratulations, and some deputations from the county.

At noon, therefore, preparatively preceded by Mr. Putney Giles, whose thought was never asleep, and whose eye was on everything, the guardians, the Cardinal and the Earl of Culloden, waited on Lothair to accompany him to his assembled friends, and, as it were, launch him into the world.

They were assembled at one end of the chief

gallery, and in a circle. Although the deputations would have to advance the whole length of the chamber, Lothair and his guardians entered from a side apartment. Even with this assistance he felt very nervous. There was no lack of feeling, and, among many, of deep feeling, on this occasion, but there was an equal and a genuine exhibition of ceremony.

The Lord Lieutenant was the first person who congratulated Lothair, though the High Sheriff had pushed forward for that purpose, but, in his awkward precipitation, he got involved with the train of the Honorable Lady Clotworthy, who bestowed on him such a withering glance, that he felt a routed man, and gave up the attempt. There were many kind and some earnest words. Even St. Aldegonde acknowledged the genius of the occasion. He was grave, graceful, and dignified, and addressing Lothair by his title he said, "that he hoped he would meet in life that happiness which he felt confident he deserved." Theodora said nothing, though her lips seemed once to move; but she retained for a moment Lothair's hand, and the expression of her countenance touched his innermost heart. Lady Corisande beamed with dazzling beauty. Her countenance was joyous, radiant; her mien imperial and triumphant. She gave her hand with graceful alacrity to Lothair, and said in a hushed tone, but every word of which reached his ear, "One of the happiest hours of my life was eight o'clock this morning."

The Lord Lieutenant and the county members then retired to the other end of the gallery, and

ushered in the deputation of the magistracy of the
county, congratulating their new brother, for Lothair
had just been appointed to the bench, on his accession to his estates.   The Lord Lieutenant himself
read the address, to which Lothair replied with a
propriety all acknowledged.   Then came the address
of the Mayor and Corporation of Grandchester, of
which city Lothair was hereditary high steward; and
then that of his tenantry, which was cordial and
characteristic.   And here many were under the impression that this portion of the proceedings would
terminate; but it was not so.   There had been some
whispering between the Bishop and the Archdeacon,
and the Rev. Dionysius Smylie had, after conference
with his superiors, twice left the chamber.   It seems
that the clergy had thought fit to take this occasion
of congratulating Lothair on his great accession, and
the proportionate duties which it would fall on him
to fulfil.   The Bishop approached Lothair and addressed him in a whisper.   Lothair seemed surprised
and a little agitated, but apparently bowed assent.
Then the Bishop and his staff proceeded to the end
of the gallery and introduced a diocesan deputation,
consisting of archdeacons and rural deans, who presented to Lothair a most uncompromising address,
and begged his acceptance of a bible and prayer-
book richly bound, and borne by the Rev. Dionysius
Smylie on a cushion of velvet.

The habitual pallor of the Cardinal's countenance
became unusually wan; the cheek of Clare Arundel
was a crimson flush; Monsignore Catesby bit his
lip; Theodora looked with curious seriousness as if

she were observing the manners of a foreign country; St. Aldegonde snorted and pushed his hand
through his hair, which had been arranged in unusual order. The great body of those present, un-
aware that this deputation was unexpected, were un-
moved.

It was a trial for Lothair, and scarcely a fair
one. He was not unequal to it, and what he said
was esteemed at the moment by all parties as satisfactory; though the Archdeacon in secret conclave
afterwards observed, that he dwelt more on Religion
than on the Church, and spoke of the Church of
Christ and not of the Church of England. He
thanked them for their present of volumes which all
must reverence or respect.

While all this was taking place within the Towers,
vast bodies of people were assembling without. Besides the notables of the county and his tenantry
and their families, which drained all the neighbouring villages, Lothair had forwarded several thousand
tickets to the Mayor and Corporation of Grandchester, for distribution among their fellow-townsmen,
who were invited to dine at Muriel and partake of
the festivities of the day, and trains were hourly arriving with their eager and happy guests. The gardens were at once open for their unrestricted pleasure, but at two o'clock, according to the custom of
the county under such circumstances, Lothair held
what in fact was a levée, or rather a drawing-room,
when every person who possessed a ticket was permitted, and even invited and expected, to pass
through the whole range of the state apartments of

Muriel Towers, and at the same time pay their respects to, and make the acquaintance of, their lord.

Lothair stood with his chief friends near him, the ladies however seated, and everyone passed—farmers and townsmen and honest folk down to the stokers of the trains from Grandchester, with whose presence St. Aldegonde was much pleased, and whom he carefully addressed as they passed by.

After this great reception they all dined in pavilions in the park—one thousand tenantry by themselves and at a fixed hour; the miscellaneous multitude in a huge crimson tent, very lofty, with many flags, and in which was served a banquet that never stopped till sunset, so that in time all might be satisfied; the notables and deputations, with the guests in the house, lunched in the armoury. It was a bright day, and there was unceasing music.

In the course of the afternoon, Lothair visited the pavilions, where his health was proposed and pledged—in the first by one of his tenants, and in the other by a workman, both orators of repute; and he addressed and thanked his friends. This immense multitude, orderly and joyous, roamed about the parks and gardens, or danced on a platform which the prescient experience of Mr. Giles had provided for them in a due locality, and whiled away the pleasant hours, in expectation a little feverish of the impending fireworks, which, there was a rumour, were to be on a scale and in a style of which neither Grandchester nor the county had any tradition.

"I remember your words at Blenheim," said Lothair to Theodora. "You cannot say the present party is founded on the principle of exclusion."

In the meantime, about six o'clock, Lothair dined in his great hall with his two hundred guests at a banquet where all the resources of nature and art seemed called upon to contribute to its luxury and splendour. The ladies who had never before dined at a public dinner were particularly delighted. They were delighted by the speeches, though they had very few; they were delighted by the national anthem, all rising; particularly they were delighted by "three times three and one cheer more," and "hip, hip." It seemed to their unpractised ears like a great naval battle, or the end of the world, or anything else of unimaginable excitement, tumult, and confusion.

The Lord Lieutenant proposed Lothair's health, and dexterously made his comparative ignorance of the subject the cause of his attempting a sketch of what he hoped might be the character of the person whose health he proposed. Everyone intuitively felt the resemblance was just and even complete, and Lothair confirmed their kind and sanguine anticipations by his terse and well-considered reply. His proposition of the ladies' healths was a signal that the carriages were ready to take them, as arranged, to Muriel Mere.

The sun had set in glory over the broad expanse of waters still glowing in the dying beam; the people were assembled in thousands on the borders of the lake, in the centre of which was an island with a pavilion. Fanciful barges and gondolas of various shapes and colours were waiting for Lothair and his party, to carry them over to the pavilion, where they found a repast which became the hour and the scene —coffee and ices and whimsical drinks, which sultanas would sip in Arabian tales. No sooner were they seated than the sound of music was heard— distant, but now nearer, till there came floating on the lake, until it rested before the pavilion, a gigantic shell, larger than the building itself, but holding in its golden and opal seats Signor Mardoni and all his orchestra.

Then came a concert rare in itself, but ravishing in the rosy twilight; and in about half an hour, when the rosy twilight had subsided into a violet eve, and when the white moon that had only gleamed began to glitter, the colossal shell again moved on, and Lothair and his companions embarking once more in their gondolas, followed it in procession about the lake. He carried in his own barque the Duchess, Theodora, and the Lord Lieutenant, and was rowed by a crew in Venetian dresses. As he handed Theodora to her seat the impulse was ir- resistible—he pressed her hand to his lips.

Suddenly a rocket rose with a hissing rush from the pavilion. It was instantly responded to from every quarter of the lake. Then the island seemed on fire, and the scene of their late festivity became a brilliant palace, with pediments and columns and statues, bright in the blaze of coloured flame. For half an hour the sky seemed covered with blue lights and the bursting forms of many-coloured stars; golden fountains, like the eruption of a marine vol- cano, rose from different parts of the water; the statued palace on the island changed and became a forest glowing with green light; and finally a temple of cerulean tint, on which appeared in huge letters of prismatic colour the name of Lothair.

The people cheered, but even the voice of the people was overcome by troops of rockets rising from every quarter of the lake, and by the thunder of artillery. When the noise and the smoke had both subsided, the name of Lothair still legible on the temple but the letters quite white, it was perceived that on every height for fifty miles round they had fired a beacon.

CHAPTER II.

THE ball at Muriel which followed the concert on the lake was one of those balls which, it would seem, never would end. All the preliminary festivities, instead of exhausting the guests of Lothair, appeared only to have excited them, and rendered them more romantic and less tolerant of the routine of existence. They danced in the great gallery, which was brilliant and crowded, and they danced as they dance in a festive dream, with joy and the enthusiasm of gaiety. The fine ladies would sanction no exclusiveness. They did not confine their inspiring society, as is sometimes too often the case, to the Brecons and the Bertrams and the Carisbrookes; they danced fully and freely with the youth of the county, and felt that in so doing they were honouring and gratifying their host.

At one o'clock they supped in the armoury, which was illuminated for the first time, and a banquet in a scene so picturesque and.resplendent renovated not merely their physical energies. At four o'clock the Duchess and a few others quietly disappeared, but her daughters remained, and St. Aldegonde danced endless reels, which was a form in which he preferred to worship Terpsichore. Perceiving by an open window that it was dawn, he came up to Lothair and said, "This is a case of breakfast."

Happy and frolicsome suggestion! The invitations circulated, and it was soon known that they were all to gather at the matin meal.

"I am so sorry that her Grace has retired," said Hugo Bohun to Lady St. Aldegonde, as he fed her with bread and butter, "because she always likes early breakfasts in the country."

The sun was shining as the guests of the house retired, and sank into couches from which it seemed they never could rise again; but, long after this, the shouts of servants and the scuffle of carriages intimated that the company in general were not so fortunate and expeditious in their retirement from the scene; and the fields were all busy, and even the towns awake, when the great body of the wearied but delighted wassailers returned from celebrating the majority of Lothair.

In the vast and statesmanlike programme of the festivities of the week, which had been prepared by Mr. and Mrs. Putney Giles, something of interest and importance had been appropriated to the morrow, but it was necessary to erase all this; and for a simple reason—no human being on the morrow morn even appeared—one might say, even stirred. After all the gay tumult in which even thousands had joined, Muriel Towers on the morrow presented a scene which only could have been equalled by the castle in the fairy tale inhabited by the Sleeping Beauty.

At length, about two hours after noon, bells began to sound which were not always answered. Then a languid household prepared a meal of which no one for a time partook, till at last a Monsignore appeared and a rival Anglican or two. Then St. Aldegonde came in with a troop of men who had been bathing in the mere, and called loudly for kidneys, which happened to be the only thing not at hand, as is always the case. St. Aldegonde always required kidneys when he had sate up all night and bathed. "But the odd thing is," he said, "you never can get anything to eat in these houses. Their infernal cooks spoil everything. That is why I hate staying with Bertha's people in the north at the end of the year. What I want in November is a slice of cod and a beefsteak, and by Jove I never could get them; I was obliged to come to town. It is no joke to have to travel three hundred miles for a slice of cod and a beefsteak."

Notwithstanding all this, however, such is the magic of custom, that by sunset civilisation had resumed its reign at Muriel Towers. The party were assembled before dinner in the saloon, and really looked as fresh and bright as if the exhausting and tumultuous yesterday had never happened. The dinner, too, notwithstanding the criticism of St. Aldegonde, was firstrate, and pleased palates not so simply fastidious as his own. The Bishop and his suite were to depart on the morrow, but the Cardinal was to remain. His Eminence talked much to Mrs. Campian, by whom, from the first, he was much struck. He was aware that she was born a Roman, and was not surprised that, having married a citizen of the United States, her sympathies were what are styled liberal; but this only stimulated his anxious resolution to accomplish her conversion, both religious and political. He recognised in her a being whose intelligence, imagination, and grandeur of character might be of invaluable service to the Church.

In the evening Monsieur Raphael and his sister, and their colleagues, gave a representation which was extremely well done. There was no theatre at Muriel, but Apollonia had felicitously arranged a contiguous saloon for the occasion, and, as everybody was at ease in an arm-chair, they all agreed it was preferable to a regular theatre.

On the morrow they were to lunch with the Mayor and Corporation of Grandchester and view some of the principal factories; on the next day the county gave a dinner to Lothair in their hall, the Lord Lieutenant in the chair; on Friday there was to be a ball at Grandchester given by the county and city united to celebrate the great local event. It was whispered that this was to be a considerable

affair. There was not an hour of the week that was
not appropriated to some festive ceremony.

It happened on the morning of Friday, the
Cardinal being alone with Lothair, transacting some
lingering business connected with the guardianship,
and on his legs as he spoke, that he said, "We live
in such a happy tumult here, my dear child, that I
have never had an opportunity of speaking to you
on one or two points which interest me and should
not be uninteresting to you. I remember a pleasant
morning-walk we had in the park at Vauxe, when
we began a conversation which we never finished.
What say you to a repetition of our stroll? 'Tis a
lovely day, and I dare say we might escape by this
window, and gain some green retreat without anyone
disturbing us."

"I am quite of your Eminence's mind," said
Lothair, taking up a wide-awake, "and I will lead
you where it is not likely we shall be disturbed."

So winding their way through the pleasure-
grounds, they entered by a wicket a part of the
park where the sunny glades soon wandered among
the tall fern and wild groves of venerable oaks.

"I sometimes feel," said the Cardinal, "that I
may have been too punctilious in avoiding conversation with you on a subject the most interesting and
important to man. But I felt a delicacy in exerting
my influence as a guardian on a subject my relations
to which, when your dear father appointed me to
that office, were so different from those which now
exist. But you are now your own master; I can use
no control over you but that influence which the

words of truth must always exercise over an ingenuous mind."

His Eminence paused for a moment and looked at his companion; but Lothair remained silent, with his eyes fixed upon the ground.

"It has always been a source of satisfaction, I would even say consolation, to me," resumed the Cardinal, "to know you were a religious man; that your disposition was reverential, which is the highest order of temperament, and brings us nearest to the angels. But we live in times of difficulty and danger —extreme difficulty and danger; a religious disposition may suffice for youth in the tranquil hour, and he may find, in due season, his appointed resting-place: but these are days of imminent peril; the soul requires a sanctuary. Is yours at hand?"

The Cardinal paused, and Lothair was obliged to meet a direct appeal. He said then, after a momentary hesitation, "When you last spoke to me, sir, on these grave matters, I said I was in a state of great despondency. My situation now is not so much despondent as perplexed."

"And I wish you to tell me the nature of your perplexity," replied the Cardinal, "for there is no anxious embarrassment of mind which Divine truth cannot disentangle and allay."

"Well," said Lothair, "I must say I am often perplexed at the differences which obtrude themselves between Divine truth and human knowledge."

"Those are inevitable," said the Cardinal. "Divine truth being unchangeable, and human knowledge changing every century; rather, I should say, every generation."

"Perhaps, instead of human knowledge, I should have said human progress," rejoined Lothair.

"Exactly," said the Cardinal, "but what is progress? Movement. But what if it be movement in the wrong direction? What if it be a departure from Divine truth?"

"But I cannot understand why religion should be inconsistent with civilisation," said Lothair.

"Religion is civilisation," said the Cardinal; "the highest: it is a reclamation of man from savageness by the Almighty. What the world calls civilisation, as distinguished from religion, is a retrograde movement, and will ultimately lead us back to the barbarism from which we have escaped. For instance, you talk of progress, what is the chief social movement of all the countries that three centuries ago separated from the unity of the Church of Christ? The rejection of the sacrament of Christian matrimony. The introduction of the law of divorce, which is, in fact, only a middle term to the abolition of marriage. What does that mean? The extinction of the home and the household on which God has rested civilisation. If there be no home, the child belongs to the state, not to the parent. The state educates the child, and without religion, because the state in a country of progress acknowledges no religion. For every man is not only to think as he likes, but to write and to speak as he likes, and to sow with both hands broadcast where he will, errors, heresies, and blasphemies, without any authority on earth to restrain the scattering of this seed of universal desolation. And this system, which would substitute for domestic sentiment and Divine belief the unlimited and licentious action of human intellect and human will, is called progress. What is it but a revolt against God!"

"I am sure I wish there were only one Church and one religion," said Lothair.

"There is only one Church and only one religion," said the Cardinal; "all other forms and phrases are mere phantasms, without root, or substance, or coherency. Look at that unhappy Germany, once so proud of its Reformation. What they call the leading journal tells us to-day, that it is a question there whether four-fifths or three-fourths of the population believe in Christianity. Some portion of it has already gone back, I understand, to NUMBER NIP. Look at this unfortunate land, divided, subdivided, parcelled out in infinite schism, with new oracles every day, and each more distinguished for the narrowness of his intellect or the loudness of his lungs; once the land of saints and scholars, and people in pious pilgrimages, and finding always solace and support in the divine offices of an ever-present Church, which were a true though a faint type of the beautiful future that awaited man. Why, only three centuries of this rebellion against the Most High have produced throughout the world, on the subject the most important that man should possess a clear, firm faith, an anarchy of opinion throwing out every monstrous and fantastic form, from a

2 *

caricature of the Greek philosophy to a revival of Fetism."

"It is a chaos," said Lothair, with a sigh.

"From which I wish to save you," said the Cardinal, with some eagerness. "This is not a time to hesitate. You must be for God, or for Antichrist. The Church calls upon her children."

"I am not unfaithful to the Church," said Lothair, "which was the Church of my fathers."

"The Church of England," said the Cardinal. "It was mine. I think of it ever with tenderness and pity. Parliament made the Church of England, and Parliament will unmake the Church of England. The Church of England is not the Church of the English. Its fate is sealed. It will soon become a sect, and all sects are fantastic. It will adopt new dogmas, or it will abjure old ones; anything to distinguish it from the non-conforming herd in which, nevertheless, it will be its fate to merge. The only consoling hope is that, when it falls, many of its children, by the aid of the Blessed Virgin, may return to Christ."

"What I regret, sir," said Lothair, "is that the Church of Rome should have placed itself in antagonism with political liberty. This adds to the difficulties which the religious cause has to encounter; for it seems impossible to deny that political freedom is now the sovereign passion of communities."

"I cannot admit," replied the Cardinal, "that the Church is in antagonism with political freedom. On the contrary, in my opinion, there can be no political freedom which is not founded on divine authority;

otherwise it can be at the best but a specious phantom of licence inevitably terminating in anarchy. The rights and liberties of the people of Ireland have no advocates except the Church; because there, political freedom is founded on Divine authority; but if you mean by political freedom the schemes of the illuminati and the freemasons which perpetually torture the Continent, all the dark conspiracies of the secret societies, there, I admit, the Church is in antagonism with such aspirations after liberty; those aspirations, in fact, are blasphemy and plunder; and if the Church were to be destroyed, Europe would be divided between the Atheist and the Communist."

There was a pause; the conversation had unexpectedly arrived at a point where neither party cared to pursue it. Lothair felt he had said enough; the Cardinal was disappointed with what Lothair had said. His Eminence felt that his late ward was not in that ripe state of probation which he had fondly anticipated; but being a man not only of vivid perception, but also of fertile resource, while he seemed to close the present conversation, he almost immediately pursued his object by another combination of means. Noticing an effect of scenery which pleased him, reminded him of Styria, and so on, he suddenly said: "You should travel."

"Well, Bertram wants me to go to Egypt with him," said Lothair.

"A most interesting country," said the Cardinal, "and well worth visiting. It is astonishing what a good guide old Herodotus still is in that land! But

you should know something of Europe before you
go there. Egypt is rather a land to end with. A
young man should visit the chief capitals of Europe,
especially the seats of learning and the arts. If my
advice were asked by a young man who contemplated travelling on a proper scale, I should say begin with Rome. Almost all that Europe contains is
derived from Rome. It is always best to go to the
fountain-head, to study the original. The society
too, there, is delightful: I know none equal to it.
That, if you please, is civilisation—pious and refined.
And the people—all so gifted and so good—so kind,
so orderly, so charitable, so truly virtuous. I believe the Roman people to be the best people that
ever lived, and this too while the secret societies
have their foreign agents in every quarter, trying to
corrupt them, but always in vain. If an act of
political violence occurs, you may be sure it is confined entirely to foreigners."

"Our friends the St. Jeromes are going to Rome,"
said Lothair.

"Well, and that would be pleasant for you.
Think seriously of this, my dear young friend. I
could be of some little service to you if you go to
Rome, which, after all, every man ought to do. I
could put you in the way of easily becoming acquainted with all the right people, who would take
care that you saw Rome with profit and advan
tage."

Just at this moment, in a winding glade, they
were met ,abruptly by a third person. All seemed
rather to start at the sudden rencounter; and then

Lothair eagerly advanced and welcomed the stranger with a proffered hand.

"This is a most unexpected, but to me most agreeable, meeting," he said. "You must now be my guest."

"That would be a great honour," said the stranger, "but one I cannot enjoy. I had to wait at the station a couple of hours or so for my train, and they told me if I strolled here I should find some pretty country. I have been so pleased with it, that I fear I have strolled too long, and I literally have not an instant at my command," and he hurried away.

"Who is that person?" asked the Cardinal with some agitation.

"I have not the slightest idea," said Lothair. "All I know is, he once saved my life."

"And all I know is," said the Cardinal, "he once threatened mine."

"Strange!" said Lothair, and then he rapidly recounted to the Cardinal his adventure at the Fenian meeting.

"Strange!" echoed his Eminence.

CHAPTER III.

Mrs. Campian did not appear at luncheon, which was observed but not noticed. Afterwards, while Lothair was making some arrangements for the amusement of his guests, and contriving that they should fit in with the chief incident of the day, which was the banquet given to him by the county, and which it was settled the ladies were not to attend, the Colonel took him aside and said, "I do not think that Theodora will care to go out to-day."

"She is not unwell, I hope?"

"Not exactly—but she has had some news, some news of some friends, which has disturbed her. And if you will excuse me, I will request your permission not to attend the dinner to-day, which I had hoped to have had the honour of doing. But I think our plans must be changed a little. I almost think we shall not go to Scotland after all."

"There is not the slightest necessity for your going to the dinner. You will have plenty to keep you in countenance at home. Lord St. Aldegonde is not going, nor I fancy any of them. I shall take the Duke with me and Lord Culloden, and if you do not go, I shall take Mr. Putney Giles. The Lord Lieutenant will meet us there. I am sorry about Mrs. Campian, because I know she is not ever put out by little things. May I not see her in the course of the day? I should be very sorry that the day should pass over without seeing her."

"Oh! I dare say she will see you in the course of the day, before you go."

"When she likes. I shall not go out to-day; I shall keep in my rooms, always at her commands. Between ourselves I shall not be sorry to have a quiet morning and collect my ideas a little. Speech-making is a new thing for me. I wish you would tell me what to say to the county."

Lothair had appropriated to the Campians one of the most convenient and complete apartments in the castle. It consisted of four chambers, one of them a saloon which had been fitted up for his mother when she married; a pretty saloon, hung with pale green silk, and portraits and scenes inlaid by Vanloo and Boucher. It was rather late in the afternoon when Lothair received a message from Theodora in reply to the wish that he had expressed of seeing her.

When he entered the room she was not seated, her countenance was serious. She advanced, and thanked him for wishing to see her, and regretted she could not receive him at an earlier hour. "I fear it may have inconvenienced you," she added; "but my mind has been much disturbed, and too agitated for conversation."

"Even now I may be an intruder?"

"No, it is past; on the contrary, I wish to speak to you; indeed, you are the only person with whom I could speak," and she sate down.

Her countenance, which was unusually pale when

he entered, became flushed. "It is not a subject for the festive hour of your life," she said, "but I cannot resist my fate."

"Your fate must always interest me," murmured Lothair.

"Yes, but my fate is the fate of ages and of nations," said Theodora, throwing up her head with that tumult of the brow which he had once before noticed. "Amid the tortures of my spirit at this moment, not the least is that there is only one person I can appeal to, and he is one to whom I have no right to make that appeal."

"If I be that person," said Lothair, "you have every right, for I am devoted to you."

"Yes; but it is not personal devotion that is the qualification needed. It is not sympathy with me that would authorise such an appeal. It must be sympathy with a cause, and a cause for which I fear you do not—perhaps I should say you cannot—feel."

"Why?" said Lothair.

"Why should you feel for my fallen country, who are the proudest citizen of the proudest of lands? Why should you feel for its debasing thraldom—you who, in the religious mystification of man, have at least the noble privilege of being a Protestant?"

"You speak of Rome?"

"Yes, of the only thought I have or ever had. I speak of that country which first impressed upon the world a general and enduring form of masculine virtue; the land of liberty, and law, and eloquence, and military genius, now garrisoned by monks and governed by a doting priest."

"Everybody must be interested about Rome," said Lothair. "Rome is the country of the world, and even the doting priest you talk of boasts of two hundred millions of subjects."

"If he were at Avignon again, I should not care for his boasts," said Theodora. "I do not grudge him his spiritual subjects; I am content to leave his superstition to Time. Time is no longer slow; his scythe mows quickly in this age. But when his debasing creeds are palmed off on man by the authority of our glorious Capitol, and the slavery of the human mind is schemed and carried on in the Forum, then, if there be real Roman blood left, and I thank my Creator there is much, it is time for it to mount and move," and she rose and walked up and down the room.

"You have had news from Rome?" said Lothair.

"I have had news from Rome," she replied, speaking slowly in a deep voice. And there was a pause.

Then Lothair said, "When you have alluded to these matters before, you never spoke of them in a sanguine spirit."

"I have seen the cause triumph," said Theodora; "the sacred cause of truth, of justice, of national honour. I have sate at the feet of the triumvirate of the Roman Republic: men who for virtue, and genius, and warlike skill and valour, and every quality that exalts man, were never surpassed

in the olden time—no, not by the Catos and the
Scipios; and I have seen the blood of my own race
poured like a rich vintage on the victorious Roman
soil: my father fell, who in stature and in mien was
a god; and, since then, my beautiful brothers, with
shapes to enshrine in temples; and I have smiled
amid the slaughter of my race, for I believed that
Rome was free; and yet all this vanished.   How
then, when we talked, could I be sanguine?"

"And yet you are sanguine now?" said Lothair,
with a scrutinising glance, and he rose and joined
her, leaning slightly on the mantel-piece.

"There was only one event that could secure
the success of our efforts," said Theodora, "and
that event was so improbable, that I had long rejected it from calculation.   It has happened, and
Rome calls upon me to act.

"The Papalini are strong," continued Theodora
after a pause; "they have been long preparing for
the French evacuation; they have a considerable and
disciplined force of Janissaries, a powerful artillery,
the strong places of the city.   The result of a rising
under such circumstances might be more than doubtful; if unsuccessful, to us it would be disastrous.   It
is necessary that the Roman States should be in-
vaded, and the Papal army must then quit their
capital.   We have no fear of them in the field.   Yes,"
she added with energy, "we could sweep them from
the face of the earth!"

"But the army of Italy," said Lothair, "will that
be inert?"

"There it is," said Theodora.   "That has been

our stumbling-block. I have always known that if ever the French quitted Rome it would be on the understanding that the house of Savoy should inherit the noble office of securing our servitude. He in whom I alone confide would never credit this, but my information in this respect was authentic. However, it is no longer necessary to discuss the question. News has come, and in no uncertain shape, that whatever may have been the understanding, under no circumstances will the Italian army enter the Roman State. We must strike, therefore, and Rome will be free. But how am I to strike? We have neither money nor arms. We have only men. I can give them no more, because I have already given them everything except my life, which is always theirs. As for my husband, who, I may say, wedded me on the battle-field, so far as wealth was concerned he was then a prince among princes, and would pour forth his treasure and his life with equal eagerness. But things have changed since Aspromonte. The struggle in his own country has entirely deprived him of revenues as great as any forfeited by their Italian princelings. In fact it is only by a chance that he is independent. Had it not been for an excellent man, one of your great English merchants, who was his agent here and managed his affairs, we should have been penniless. His judicious investments of the superfluity of our income, which at the time my husband never even noticed, have secured for Colonel Campian the means of that decorous life which he appreciates— but no more. As for myself these considerations

are nothing. I will not say I should be insensible
to a refined life with refined companions, if the
spirit were content and the heart serene; but I never
could fully realise the abstract idea of what they
call wealth; I never could look upon it except as a
means to an end, and my end has generally been
military material. Perhaps the vicissitudes of my
life have made me insensible to what are called re-
verses of fortune, for when a child I remember
sleeping on the moonlit flags of Paris, with no pillow except my tambourine, and I remember it not
without delight. Let us sit down. I feel I am
talking in an excited, injudicious, egotistical, rhap-
sodical manner. I thought I was calm and I meant
to have been clear. But the fact is I am ashamed
of myself. I am doing a wrong thing and in a
wrong manner. But I have had a sleepless night
and a day of brooding thought. I meant once to
have asked you to help me, and now I feel that
you are the last person to whom I ought to appeal."

"In that you are in error," said Lothair rising
and taking her hand with an expression of much
gravity; "I am the right person for you to appeal
to—the only person."

"Nay," said Theodora, and she shook her
head.

"For I owe to you a debt that I never can repay," continued Lothair. "Had it not been for
you, I should have remained what I was when we
first met, a prejudiced, narrow-minded being, with
contracted sympathies and false knowledge, wasting

my life on obsolete trifles, and utterly insensible to
the privilege of living in this wondrous age of
change and progress. Why, had it not been for
you I should have at this very moment been lavish-
ing my fortune on an ecclesiastical toy, which I
think of with a blush. There may be—doubtless
there are—opinions in which we may not agree;
but in our love of truth and justice there is no difference, dearest lady. No; though you must have
felt that I am not—that no one could be—insensible
to your beauty and infinite charms, still it is your
consummate character that has justly fascinated my
thought and heart; and I have long resolved, were
I permitted, to devote to you my fortune and my
life."

CHAPTER IV.

THE month of September was considerably advanced, when a cab, evidently from its luggage fresh
from the railway, entered the courtyard of Hexham
House, of which the shuttered windows indicated
the absence of its master, the Cardinal, then in
Italy. But it was evident that the person who had
arrived was expected, for before his servant could
ring the hall bell the door opened, and a grave-
looking domestic advanced with much deference,
and awaited the presence of no less a personage
than Monsignore Berwick.

"We have had a rough passage, good Clifford,"

said the great man, alighting, "but I see you duly
received my telegram. You are always ready."

"I hope my Lord will find it not uncomfortable,"
said Clifford. "I have prepared the little suite
which you mentioned, and have been careful that
there should be no outward sign of anyone having
arrived."

"And now," said the Monsignore, stopping for
a moment in the hall, "here is a letter which must
be instantly delivered and by a trusty hand," and he
gave it to Mr. Clifford, who, looking at the direction, nodded his head and said, "By no one but
myself. I will show my Lord to his rooms, and depart with this instantly."

"And bring back a reply," added the Monsignore.

The well-lit room, the cheerful fire, the judicious
refection on a side table, were all circumstances
which usually would have been agreeable to a
wearied traveller, but Monsignore Berwick seemed
little to regard them. Though a man in general
superior to care and master of thought, his countenance was troubled and pensive even to dejection.

"Even the winds and waves are against us," he
exclaimed, too restless to be seated, and walking up
and down the room with his arms behind his back.
"That such a struggle should fall to my lot! Why
was I not a minister in the days of the Gregorys,
the Innocents, even the Leos! But this is craven.
There should be inspiration in peril, and the
greatest where peril is extreme. I am a little upset
—with travel and the voyage and those telegrams

not being answered. The good Clifford was wisely
provident," and he approached the table and took
one glass of wine. "Good! One must never despair
in such a cause. And if the worse happens, it has
happened before—and what then? Suppose Avignon
over again, or even Gaeta, or even Paris? So long
as we never relinquish our title to the Eternal City
we shall be eternal. But then, some say, our enemies
before were the sovereigns; now it is the people. Is
it so? True we have vanquished kings and baffled
emperors—but the French Republic and the Roman
Republic have alike reigned and ruled in the Vatican,
and where are they? We have lost provinces, but
we have also gained them. We have twelve millions
of subjects in the United States of America, and
they will increase like the sands of the sea. Still it
is a hideous thing to have come back, as it were, to
the days of the Constable of Bourbon, and to be
contemplating the siege of the Holy See, and massacre and pillage and ineffable horrors! The Papacy
may survive such calamities, as it undoubtedly will,
but I shall scarcely figure in history if under my influence such visitations should accrue. If I had only
to deal with men I would not admit of failure; but
when your antagonists are human thoughts, represented by invisible powers, there is something that
might baffle a Machiavel and appal a Borgia."

While he was meditating in this vein the door
opened, and Mr. Clifford with some hasty action
and speaking rapidly exclaimed—

"He said he would be here sooner than myself.
His carriage was at the door. I drove back as fast

as possible—and indeed I hear something now in the court," and he disappeared.

It was only to usher in, almost immediately, a stately personage in an evening dress, and wearing a decoration of a high class, who saluted the Monsignore with great cordiality.

"I am engaged to dine with the Prussian Ambassador, who has been obliged to come to town to receive a prince of the blood who is visiting the dockyards here; but I thought you might be later than you expected, and I ordered my carriage to be in waiting, so that we have a good little hour—and I can come on to you again afterwards if that will not do."

"A little hour with us is a long hour with other people," said the Monsignore, "because we are friends and can speak without windings. You are a true friend to the Holy See; you have proved it. We are in great trouble and need of aid."

"I hear that things are not altogether as we could wish," said the gentleman in an evening dress; "but I hope, and should think, only annoyances."

"Dangers," said Berwick, "and great."

"How so?"

"Well, we have invasion threatening us without and insurrection within," said Berwick. "We might, though it is doubtful, successfully encounter one of these perils, but their united action must be fatal."

"All this has come suddenly," said the gentleman. "In the summer you had no fear, and our people wrote to us that we might be perfectly tranquil."

"Just so," said Berwick. "If we had met a month ago I should have told you the same thing. A month ago the revolution seemed lifeless, penniless; without a future, without a resource. They had no money, no credit, no men. At present, quietly but regularly, they are assembling by thousands on our frontiers; they have to our knowledge received two large consignments of small arms, and apparently have unlimited credit with the trade, both in Birmingham and Liége; they have even artillery; everything is paid for in coin or in good bills—and, worst of all, they have a man, the most consummate soldier in Europe. I thought he was at New York, and was in hopes he would never have recrossed the Atlantic—but I know that he passed through Florence a fortnight ago, and I have seen a man who says he spoke to him at Narni."

"The Italian government must stop all this," said the gentleman.

"They do not stop it," said Berwick. "The government of his Holiness has made every representation to them: we have placed in their hands indubitable evidence of the illegal proceedings that are taking place and of the internal dangers we experience in consequence of their exterior movements. But they do nothing: it is even believed that the royal troops are joining the insurgents, and Garibaldi is spouting with impunity in every balcony of Florence."

"You may depend upon it that our government is making strong representations to the government of Florence."

"I come from Paris and elsewhere," said Berwick with animation and perhaps a degree of impatience. "I have seen everybody there, and I have heard everything. It is not representations that are wanted from your government; it is something of a different kind."

"But if you have seen everybody at Paris and heard everything, how can I help you?"

"By acting upon the government here. A word from you to the English Minister would have great weight at this juncture. Queen Victoria is interested in the maintenance of the Papal throne. Her Catholic subjects are counted by millions. The influence of his Holiness has been hitherto exercised against the Fenians. France would interfere if she was sure the step would not be disapproved by England."

"Interfere!" said the gentleman. "Our return to Rome almost before we have paid our laundresses' bills in the Eternal City would be a diplomatic scandal."

"A diplomatic scandal would be preferable to a European revolution."

"Suppose we were to have both?" and the gentleman drew his chair near the fire.

"I am convinced that a want of firmness now," said Berwick, "would lead to inconceivable calamities for all of us."

"Let us understand each other, my very dear friend Berwick," said his companion, and he threw his arm over the back of his chair and looked the Roman full in his face. "You say you have been at Paris and elsewhere, and have seen everybody and heard everything."

"Yes, yes."

"Something has happened to us also during the last month, and as unexpectedly as to yourselves."

"The secret societies? Yes, he spoke to me on that very point, and fully. 'Tis strange, but is only, in my opinion, an additional argument in favour of crushing the evil influence."

"Well, that he must decide. But the facts are startling. A month ago the secret societies in France were only a name; they existed only in the memory of the police, and almost as a tradition. At present we know that they are in complete organisation, and what is most strange is, that the prefects write they have information that the Mary-Anne associations, which are essentially republican and are scattered about the provinces, are all revived, and are astir. MARY-ANNE, as you know, was the red name for the Republic years ago, and there always was a sort of myth that these societies had been founded by a woman. Of course that is all nonsense, but they keep it up; it affects the public imagination, and my government has undoubted evidence that the word of command has gone round to all these societies that Mary-Anne has returned and will issue her orders, which must be obeyed."

"The Church is stronger, and especially in the provinces, than the Mary-Anne societies," said Berwick.

"I hope so," said his friend; "but you see, my

dear Monsignore, the question with us is not so
simple as you put it. The secret societies will not
tolerate another Roman interference, to say nothing
of the diplomatic hubbub, which we might, if necessary, defy; but what if, taking advantage of the
general indignation, your new kingdom of Italy may
seize the golden opportunity of making a popular
reputation, and declare herself the champion of national independence against the interference of the
foreigner? My friend, we tread on delicate ground."

"If Rome falls, not an existing dynasty in Europe will survive five years," said Berwick.

"It may be so," said his companion, but with
no expression of incredulity. "You know how con-
sistently and anxiously I have always laboured to
support the authority of the Holy See, and to maintain its territorial position as the guarantee of its
independence; but fate has decided against us. I
cannot indulge in the belief that his Holiness will
ever regain his lost provinces; a capital without a
country is an apparent anomaly, which I fear will
always embarrass us. We can treat the possession
as the capital of Christendom, but, alas! all the
world are not as good Christians as ourselves, and
Christendom is a country no longer marked out in
the map of the world. I wish," continued the
gentleman in a tone almost coaxing—"I wish we
could devise some plan which, humanly speaking,
would secure to his Holiness the possession of his
earthly throne for ever. I wish I could induce you
to consider more favourably that suggestion, that his
Holiness should content himself with the ancient

city, and, in possession of St. Peter's and the Vatican, leave the rest of Rome to the vulgar cares and the mundane anxieties of the transient generation. Yes," he added with energy, "if, my dear Berwick, you could see your way to this, or something like this, I think even now and at once, I could venture to undertake that the Emperor, my master, would soon put an end to all these disturbances and dangers, and that——"

"Non possumus," said Berwick, sternly stopping him, "sooner than that Attila, the Constable of Bourbon, or the blasphemous orgies of the Red Republic! After all, it is the Church against the secret societies. They are the only two strong things in Europe, and will survive kings, emperors, or parliaments."

At this moment there was a tap at the door, and, bidden to enter, Mr. Clifford presented himself with a sealed paper for the gentleman in evening dress. Your secretary, sir, brought this, which he said must be given you before you went to the Ambassador."

"'Tis well," said the gentleman, and he rose, and with a countenance of some excitement read the paper, which contained a telegram; and then he said, "This, I think, will help us out of our immediate difficulties, my dear Monsignore. Rattazzi has behaved like a man of sense and has arrested Garibaldi. But you do not seem, my friend, as pleased as I should have anticipated."

"Garibaldi has been arrested before," said Berwick.

"Well, well, I am hopeful; but I must go to my dinner. I will see you again to-morrow."

CHAPTER V.

THE continuous gathering of what, in popular language, were styled the Garibaldi Volunteers, on the southern border of the Papal territory in the autumn of 1867, was not the only or perhaps the greatest danger which then threatened the Holy See, though the one which most attracted its alarmed attention. The considerable numbers in which this assemblage was suddenly occurring; the fact that the son of the Liberator had already taken its command, and only as the precursor of his formidable sire; the accredited rumour that Ghirelli at the head of a purely Roman legion was daily expected to join the frontier force; that Nicotera was stirring in the old Neapolitan kingdom, while the Liberator himself at Florence and in other parts of Tuscany was even ostentatiously, certainly with impunity, preaching the new crusade and using all his irresistible influence with the populace to excite their sympathies and to stimulate their energy, might well justify the extreme apprehension of the court of Rome. And yet dangers at least equal, and almost as close, were at the same time preparing unnoticed and unknown.

In the mountainous range between Fiascone and Viterbo, contiguous to the sea, is a valley surrounded by chains of steep and barren hills, but which is

watered by a torrent scarcely dry even in summer;
so that the valley itself, which is not inconsiderable
in its breadth, is never without verdure, while almost
a forest of brushwood formed of shrubs, which in
England we should consider rare, bounds the natural
turf and ascends sometimes to no inconsiderable
height the nearest hills.

Into this valley, towards the middle of September,
there defiled one afternoon through a narrow pass
a band of about fifty men, all armed, and conducting a cavalcade or rather a caravan of mules laden
with munitions of war and other stores. When they
had gained the centre of the valley and a general
halt was accomplished, their commander, accompanied by one who was apparently an officer, surveyed all the points of the locality; and when their
companions had rested and refreshed themselves,
they gave the necessary orders for the preparation
of a camp. The turf already afforded a sufficient
area for their present wants, but it was announced
that on the morrow they must commence clearing
the brushwood. In the mean time, one of the live-
liest scenes of military life soon rapidly developed
itself: the canvass houses were pitched, the sentries
appointed, the videttes established. The commissariat was limited to bread and olives and generally
the running stream, varied sometimes by coffee and
always consoled by tobacco.

On the third day, amidst their cheerful though
by no means light labours, a second caravan arrived,
evidently expected and heartily welcomed. Then in
another eight-and-forty hours, smaller bodies of men

seemed to drop down from the hills, generally without stores, but always armed. Then men came from neighbouring islands in open boats, and one morning a considerable detachment crossed the water from Corsica. So that at the end of a week or ten days there was an armed force of several hundred men in this once silent valley, now a scene of constant stir and continual animation, for some one or something was always arriving, and from every quarter; men and arms and stores crept in from every wild pass of the mountains and every little rocky harbour of the coast.

About this time, while the officer in command was reviewing a considerable portion of the troops, the rest labouring in still clearing the brushwood and establishing the many works incidental to a camp, half a dozen horsemen were seen descending the mountain pass by which the original body had entered the valley. A scout had preceded them, and the troops with enthusiasm awaited the arrival of that leader, a message from whose magic name had summoned them to this secluded rendezvous from many a distant state and city. Unruffled, but with an inspiring fire in his pleased keen eye, that General answered their devoted salute whom hitherto we have known by his travelling name of Captain Bruges.

It was only towards the end of the preceding month that he had resolved to take the field; but the organisation of the secret societies is so complete that he knew he could always almost instantly secure the assembling of a picked force in a particular place. The telegraph circulated its mystic messages to every part of France and Italy and Belgium, and to some old friends not so conveniently at hand, but who he doubted not would arrive in due time for action. He himself had employed the interval in forwarding all necessary supplies, and he had passed through Florence in order that he might confer with the great spirit of Italian movement and plan with him the impending campaign.

After he had passed in review the troops, the General, with the officers of his staff who had accompanied him, visited on foot every part of the camp. Several of the men he recognised by name; to all of them he addressed some inspiring word; a memory of combats in which they had fought together, or happy allusions to adventures of romantic peril; some question which indicated that local knowledge which is magical for those who are away from home; mixed with all this, sharp, clear enquiries as to the business of the hour, which proved the master of detail, severe in discipline but never deficient in sympathy for his troops.

After sunset, enveloped in their cloaks, the General and his companions, the party increased by the officers who had been in command previous to his arrival, smoked their cigars round the camp fire.

"Well, Sarano," said the General, "I will look over your muster-roll to-morrow, but I should suppose I may count on a thousand rifles or so. I want three, and we shall get them. The great man would have supplied them me at once, but I will not have boys. He must send those on to Menotti. I told him, 'I am not a man of genius; I do not pretend to conquer kingdoms with boys. Give me old soldiers, men who have served a couple of campaigns, and been seasoned with four-and-twenty months of camp life, and I will not disgrace you or myself.'"

"We have had no news from the other place for a long time," said Sarano. "How is it?"

"Well enough. They are in the mountains about Nerola, in a position not very unlike this; numerically strong, for Nicotera has joined them, and Ghirelli with the Roman Legion is at hand. They must be quiet till the great man joins them; I am told they are restless. There has been too much noise about the whole business. Had they been as mum as you have been, we should not have had all these representations from France and these threatened difficulties from that quarter. The Papalini would have complained and remonstrated, and Rattazzi could have conscientiously assured the people at Paris that they were dealing with exaggerations and bugbears; the very existence of the frontier force would have become a controversy, and while the newspapers were proving it was a myth we should have been in the Vatican."

"And when shall we be there, General?"

"I do not want to move for a month. By that time I shall have two thousand five hundred or three thousand of my old comrades, and the great man will have put his boys in trim. Both bodies must leave their mountains at the same time, join in the open country and march to Rome."

As the night advanced, several of the party rose and left the camp fire—some to their tents, some to their duties. Two of the staff remained with the General.

"I am disappointed and uneasy that we have not heard from Paris," said one of them.

"I am disappointed," said the General, "but not uneasy; she never makes a mistake."

"The risk was too great," rejoined the speaker in a depressed tone.

"I do not see that," said the General. "What is the risk? Who could possibly suspect the lady's maid of the Princess of Tivoli! I am told that the Princess has become quite a favourite at the Tuileries."

"They say that the police is not so well informed as it used to be; nevertheless, I confess I should be much happier were she sitting round this camp fire."

"Courage!" said the General. "I do not believe in many things, but I do believe in the divine Theodora. What say you, Captain Muriel? I hope you are not offended by my criticism of young soldiers. You are the youngest in our band, but you have good military stuff in you, and will be soon seasoned."

"I feel I serve under a master of the art," replied Lothair, "and will not take the gloomy view of Colonel Campian about our best friend, though I share all his disappointment. It seems to me that

detection is impossible. I am sure that I could not
have recognised her when I handed the Princess
into her carriage."

"The step was absolutely necessary," said the
General; "no one could be trusted but herself—no
other person has the influence. All our danger is
from France. The Italian troops will never cross
the frontier to attack us, rest assured of that. I
have proof of it. And it is most difficult, almost
impossible, for the French to return. There never
would have been an idea of such a step, if there had
been a little more discretion at Florence, less of
those manifestoes and speeches from balconies. But
we must not criticise one who is above criticism.
Without him we could do nothing, and when he
stamps his foot men rise from the earth. I will go
the rounds; come with me, Captain Muriel. Colonel,
I order you to your tent; you are a veteran—the
only one among us, at least on the staff, who was
wounded at Aspromonte."

CHAPTER VL

THE life of Lothair had been so strange and
exciting since he quitted Muriel Towers that he had
found little time for that reflection in which he was
once so prone to indulge. Perhaps he shrank from
it. If he wanted an easy distraction from self-criti-
cism—it may be a convenient refuge from the
scruples, or even the pangs, of conscience—it was

profusely supplied by the startling affairs of which he formed a part, the singular characters with whom he was placed in contact, the risk and responsibility which seemed suddenly to have encompassed him with their ever-stimulating influence, and, lastly, by the novelty of foreign travel, which even under ordinary circumstances has a tendency to rouse and stir up even ordinary men.

So long as Theodora was his companion in their councils and he was listening to her deep plans and daring suggestions, enforced by that calm enthusiasm which was not the least powerful of her commanding spells, it is not perhaps surprising that he should have yielded without an effort to her bewitching ascendency. But when they had separated, and she had embarked on that perilous enterprise of personally conferring with the chiefs of those secret societies of France which had been fancifully baptised by her popular name and had nurtured her tradition as a religious faith, it might have been supposed that Lothair, left to himself, might have recurred to the earlier sentiments of his youth. But he was not left to himself. He was left with her injunctions, and the spirit of the oracle, though the divinity was no longer visible, pervaded his mind and life.

Lothair was to accompany the General as one of his aides-de-camp, and he was to meet Theodora again on what was contemplated as the field of memorable actions. Theodora had wisely calculated on the influence, beneficial in her view, which the character of a man like the General would exercise over Lothair. This consummate military leader,

though he had pursued a daring career and was a
man of strong convictions, was distinguished by an
almost unerring judgment and a mastery of method
rarely surpassed.   Though he was without imagination or sentiment there were occasions on which he
had shown he was not deficient in a becoming sympathy, and he had a rapid and correct perception of
character.   He was a thoroughly honest man, and
in the course of a life of great trial and vicissitude
even envenomed foes had never impeached his pure
integrity.   For the rest, he was unselfish, but severe
in discipline, inflexible, and even ruthless in the fulfilment of his purpose.   A certain simplicity of
speech and conduct, and a disinterestedness which
even in little things was constantly exhibiting itself,
gave to his character even charm, and rendered personal intercourse with him highly agreeable.

In the countless arrangements which had to be
made, Lothair was never wearied in recognising and
admiring the prescience and precision of his chief;
and when the day had died, and for a moment they
had ceased from their labours, or were travelling
together, often through the night, Lothair found in
the conversation of his companion, artless and un-
restrained, a wonderful fund of knowledge both of
men and things, and that, too, in very different
climes and countries.

The camp in the Apennines was not favourable
to useless reverie.   Lothair found unceasing and
deeply interesting occupation in his numerous and
novel duties, and if his thoughts for a moment wandered beyond the barren peaks around him they

were attracted and engrossed by one subject—and that was, naturally, Theodora. From her they had heard nothing since her departure, except a mysterious though not discouraging telegram which was given to them by Colonel Campian when he had joined them at Florence. It was difficult not to feel anxious about her, though the General would never admit the possibility of her personal danger.

In this state of affairs, a week having elapsed since his arrival at the camp, Lothair, who had been visiting the outposts, was summoned one morning by an orderly to the tent of the General. That personage was on his legs when Lothair entered it, and was dictating to an officer writing at a table.

"You ought to know my military secretary," said the General as Lothair entered, "and therefore I will introduce you."

Lothair was commencing a suitable reverence of recognition as the secretary raised his head to receive it, when he suddenly stopped, changed colour, and for a moment seemed to lose himself, and then murmured, "Is it possible?"

It was indeed Theodora: clothed in male attire she seemed a stripling.

"Quite possible," she said, "and all is well. But I found it a longer business than I had counted on. You see, there are so many new persons who knew me only by tradition, but with whom it was necessary I should personally confer. And I had more difficulty, just now, in getting through Florence than I had anticipated. The Papalini and the French are both worrying our allies in that city

about the gathering on the southern frontier, and
there is a sort of examination, true or false I will
not aver, of all who depart. However, I managed
to pass with some soldiers' wives who were carrying
fruit as far as Narni, and there I met an old comrade of Aspromonte, who is a custom-officer now,
but true to the good cause, and he, and his daughter
who is with me, helped me through everything, and
so I am with my dear friends again."

After some slight conversation in this vein
Theodora entered into a detailed narrative of her
proceedings, and gave to them her views of the condition of affairs.

"By one thing, above all others," she said, "I
am impressed, and that is the unprecedented efforts
which Rome is making to obtain the return of the
French. There never was such influence exercised,
such distinct offers made, such prospects intimated.
You may prepare yourself for anything; a papal
coronation, a family pontiff—I could hardly say a
king of Rome, though he has been reminded of that
royal fact. Our friends have acted with equal
energy and with perfect temper. The heads of the
societies have met in council, and resolved that if
France will refuse to interfere no domestic disturbance shall be attempted during this reign, and
they have communicated this resolution to head-
quarters. He trusts them; he knows they are honest
men. They did something like this before the
Italian war, when he hesitated about heading the
army from the fear of domestic revolution. Anxious
to secure the freedom of Italy, they apprised him

that if he personally entered the field they would
undertake to ensure tranquillity at home. The engagement was scrupulously fulfilled. When I left
Paris all looked well, but affairs require the utmost
vigilance and courage. It is a mighty struggle; it
is a struggle between the Church and the secret
societies; and it is a death struggle."

CHAPTER VII.

DURING the week that elapsed after the arrival
of Theodora at the camp, many recruits and considerable supplies of military stores reached the
valley. Theodora really acted as secretary to the
General, and her labours were not light. Though
Lothair was frequently in her presence, they were
never or rarely alone, and when they conversed together her talk was of details. The scouts, too,
had brought information, which might have been
expected, that their rendezvous was no longer a
secret at Rome. The garrison of the neighbouring
town of Viterbo had therefore been increased, and
there was even the commencement of an entrenched
camp in the vicinity of that place, to be garrisoned
by a detachment of the legion of Antibes and other
good troops, so that any junction between the
General and Garibaldi, if contemplated, should not
be easily effected.

In the meantime, the life of the camp was busy.
The daily drill and exercise of two thousand men

4*

was not a slight affair, and the constant changes in
orders which the arrival of bodies of recruits occasioned rendered this primary duty more difficult;
the office of quarter-master required the utmost resource and temper; the commissariat, which from
the nature of the country could depend little upon
forage, demanded extreme husbandry and forbear-
ance.   But perhaps no labours were more severe
than those of the armourers, the clink of whose instruments resounded unceasingly in the valley. And
yet such is the magic of method, when directed by
a master mind, that the whole went on with the
regularity and precision of machinery.   More than
two thousand armed men, all of whom had been
accustomed to an irregular, some to a lawless life,
were as docile as children; animated, in general,
by what they deemed a sacred cause, and led by
a chief whom they universally alike adored and
feared.

Among these wild warriors, Theodora, delicate
and fragile, but with a mien of majesty, moved like
the spirit of some other world, and was viewed
by them with admiration not unmixed with awe.
Veterans round the camp fire had told to the new
recruits her deeds of prowess and devotion; how
triumphantly she had charged at Voltorno, and how
heroically she had borne their standard when they
were betrayed at fatal Aspromonte.

The sun had sunk behind the mountains, but
was still high in the western heaven, when a mounted
lancer was observed descending a distant pass into
the valley.   The General and his staff had not long

commenced their principal meal of the day, of which the disappearance of the sun behind the peak was the accustomed signal. This permitted them, without inconvenience, to take their simple repast in the open, but still warm, air. Theodora was seated between the General and her husband, and her eye was the first that caught the figure of the distant but descending stranger.

"What is that?" she asked.

The General immediately using his telescope, after a moment's examination, said—

"A lancer of the Royal Guard."

All eyes were now fixed upon the movements of the horseman. He had descended the winding steep and now was tracking the craggy path which led into the plain. As he reached the precinct of the camp he was challenged but not detained. Nearer and nearer he approached, and it was evident from his uniform that the conjecture of his character by the General was correct.

"A deserter from the Guard," whispered Colonel Campian to Lothair.

The horseman was conducted by an officer to the presence of the commander. When that presence was reached the lancer, still silent, slowly lowered his tall weapon and offered the General the despatch which was fastened to the head of his spear.

Every eye was on the countenance of their chief as he perused the missive, but that countenance was always inscrutable. It was observed, however, that he read the paper twice. Looking up, the General said to the officer: "See that the bearer is well

quartered. This is for you," he added in a low
voice to Theodora, and he gave her an enclosure;
"read it quietly, and then come into my tent."

Theodora read the letter, and quietly; though,
without the preparatory hint, it might have been difficult to have concealed her emotion.   Then, after
a short pause, she rose, and the General, requesting
his companions not to disturb themselves, joined her,
and they proceeded in silence to his tent.

"He is arrested," said the General when they
had entered it, "and taken to Alessandria, where
he is a close prisoner. 'Tis a blow, but I am more
grieved than surprised."

This was the arrest of Garibaldi at Sinigaglia by
the Italian government, which had been communicated at Hexham House to Monsignore Berwick by
his evening visitor.

"How will it affect operations in the field?" enquired Theodora.

"According to this despatch, in no degree. Our
original plan is to be pursued, and acted upon the
moment we are ready. That should be in a fortnight, or perhaps three weeks. Menotti is to take
the command on the southern frontier.   Well, it
may prevent jealousies. I think I shall send Sarano
there to reconnoitre; he is well both with Nicotera
and Ghirelli, and may keep things straight."

"But there are other affairs besides operations
in the field," said Theodora, "and scarcely less
critical. Read this," and she gave him the enclosure,
which ran in these words:—

"The General will tell thee what has happened. Have no fear for that. All will go right. It will not alter our plans a bunch of grapes. Be perfectly easy about this country. No Italian soldier will ever cross the frontier except to combat the French. Write that on thy heart. Are other things as well? other places? My advices are bad. All the prelates are on their knees to him—with blessings on their lips and curses in their pockets. Archbishop of Paris is as bad as any. Berwick is at Biarritz—an inexhaustible intriguer; the only priest I fear. I hear from one who never misled me that the Polhes brigade has orders to be in readiness. The MARY-ANNE societies are not strong enough for the situation—too local; he listens to them, but he has given no pledge. We must go deeper. 'Tis an affair of 'MADRE NATURA.' Thou must see Colonna."

"Colonna is at Rome," said the General, "and cannot be spared. He is acting President of the National Committee, and has enough upon his hands."

"I must see him," said Theodora.

"I had hoped I had heard the last of the 'Madre Natura,'" said the General with an air of discontent.

"And the Neapolitans hope they have heard the last of the eruptions of their mountain," said Theodora; "but the necessities of things are sterner stuff than the hopes of men."

"Its last effort appalled and outraged Europe," said the General.

"Its last effort forced the French into Italy, and

has freed the country from the Alps to the Adriatic,"
rejoined Theodora.

"If the great man had only been as quiet as we
have been," said the General, lighting a cigar, "we
might have been in Rome by this time."

"If the great man had been quiet, we should
not have had a volunteer in our valley," said Theodora. "My faith in him is implicit; he has been
right in everything, and has never failed except
when he has been betrayed. I see no hope for
Rome except in his convictions and energy. I do
not wish to die and feel I have devoted my life only
to secure the triumph of Savoyards who have sold
their own country, and of priests whose impostures
have degraded mine."

"Ah! those priests!" exclaimed the General.
"I really do not much care for anything else. They
say the Savoyard is not a bad comrade, and at any
rate he can charge like a soldier. But those priests!
I fluttered them once! Why did I spare any? Why
did I not burn down St. Peter's? I proposed it,
but Mirandola, with his history and his love of art
and all that old furniture, would reserve it for a
temple of the true God and for the glory of Europe!
Fine results we have accomplished! And now we
are here, hardly knowing where we are, and, as it
appears, hardly knowing what to do."

"Not so, dear General," said Theodora. "Where
we are is the threshold of Rome, and if we are wise
we shall soon cross it. This arrest of our great
friend is a misfortune, but not an irredeemable one.
I thoroughly credit what he says about the Italian

troops. Rest assured he knows what he is talking about: they will never cross the frontier against us. The danger is from another land. But there will be no peril if we are prompt and firm. Clear your mind of all these dark feelings about the MADRE NATURA. All that we require is that the most powerful and the most secret association In Europe should ratify what the local societies of France have already intimated. It will be enough. Send for Colonna, and leave the rest to me."

CHAPTER VIII.

THE "MADRE NATURA" is the oldest, the most powerful, and the most occult of the secret societies of Italy. Its mythic origin reaches the era of paganism, and it is not impossible that it may have been founded by some of the despoiled professors of the ancient faith. As time advanced, the brotherhood assumed many outward forms, according to the varying spirit of the age: sometimes they were freemasons, sometimes they were soldiers, sometimes artists, sometimes men of letters. But whether their external representation were a lodge, a commandery, a studio, or an academy, their inward purpose was ever the same; and that was to cherish the memory, and, if possible, to secure the restoration, of the Roman republic, and to expel from the Aryan settlement of Romulus the creeds and sovereignty of what they styled the Semitic invasion.

The "MADRE NATURA" have a tradition that
one of the most celebrated of the Popes was admitted to their fraternity as Cardinal dei Medici,
and that when he ascended the throne, mainly
through their labours, he was called upon to co-
operate in the fulfilment of the great idea. An
individual who in his youth has been the member
of a secret society, and subsequently ascends a
throne, may find himself in an embarrassing position.
This, however, according to the tradition, which
there is some documentary ground to accredit, was
not the perplexing lot of his Holiness, Pope Leo X.
His tastes and convictions were in entire unison
with his early engagements, and it is believed that
he took an early and no unwilling opportunity of
submitting to the conclave a proposition to consider
whether it were not both expedient and practicable
to return to the ancient faith, for which their temples
had been originally erected.

The chief tenet of the society of "MADRE NA-
TURA" is denoted by its name. They could conceive nothing more benignant and more beautiful,
more provident and more powerful, more essentially
divine, than that system of creative order to which
they owed their being, and in which it was their
privilege to exist. But they differed from other
schools of philosophy that have held this faith in
this singular particular: they recognised the inability
of the Latin race to pursue the worship of nature in
an abstract spirit, and they desired to revive those
exquisite personifications of the abounding qualities
of the mighty mother which the Aryan genius had

bequeathed to the admiration of man. Parthenope was again to rule at Naples instead of Januarius, and starveling saints and winking madonnas were to restore their usurped altars to the god of the silver bow and the radiant daughter of the foaming wave.

Although the society of "MADRE NATURA" themselves accepted the allegorical interpretation which the Neo-Platonists had placed upon the Pagan creeds during the first ages of Christianity, they could not suppose that the populace could ever comprehend an exposition so refined, not to say so fanciful. They guarded, therefore, against the corruptions and abuses of the religion of nature by the entire abolition of the priestly order, and in the principle that every man should be his own priest they believed they had found the necessary security.

As it was evident that the arrest of Garibaldi could not be kept secret, the General thought it most prudent to be himself the herald of its occurrence, which he announced to the troops in a manner as little discouraging as he could devise. It was difficult to extenuate the consequences of so great a blow, but they were assured that it was not a catastrophe, and would not in the slightest degree affect the execution of the plans previously resolved on. Two or three days later some increase of confidence was occasioned by the authentic intelligence that Garibaldi had been removed from his stern imprisonment at Alessandria, and conveyed to his island-home, Caprera, though still a prisoner.

About this time, the General said to Lothair,

"My secretary has occasion to go on an expedition. I shall send a small detachment of cavalry with her, and you will be at its head. She has requested that her husband should have this office, but that is impossible; I cannot spare my best officer. It is your first command, and though I hope it will involve no great difficulty, there is no command that does not require courage and discretion. The distance is not very great, and so long as you are in the mountains you will probably be safe; but in leaving this range and gaining the southern Apennines, which is your point of arrival, you will have to cross the open country. I do not hear the Papalini are in force there; I believe they have concentrated themselves at Rome, and about Viterbo. If you meet any scouts and reconnoitring parties, you will be able to give a good account of them, and probably they will be as little anxious to encounter you as you to meet them. But we must be prepared for everything, and you may be threatened by the enemy in force; in that case you will cross the Italian frontier, in the immediate neighbourhood of which you will keep during the passage of the open country, and surrender yourselves and your arms to the authorities. They will not be very severe; but at whatever cost and whatever may be the odds, Theodora must never be a prisoner to the Papalini. You will depart to-morrow at dawn."

There is nothing so animating, so invigorating alike to body and soul, so truly delicious, as travelling among mountains in the early hours of the day. The freshness of nature falls upon a responsive frame, and the nobility of the scene discards the petty thoughts that pester ordinary life. So felt Captain Muriel, as with every military precaution he conducted his little troop and his precious charge among the winding passes of the Apennines; at first dim in the matin twilight, then soft with incipient day, then coruscating with golden flashes. Sometimes they descended from the austere heights into the sylvan intricacies of chestnut forests, amid the rush of waters and the fragrant stir of ancient trees; and then again ascending to lofty summits, ranges of interminable hills, grey or green, expanded before them, with ever and anon a glimpse of plains, and sometimes the splendour and the odour of the sea.

Theodora rode a mule, which had been presented to the General by some admirer. It was an animal of remarkable beauty and intelligence, perfectly aware, apparently, of the importance of its present trust, and proud of its rich accoutrements, its padded saddle of crimson velvet, and its silver bells. A couple of troopers formed the advanced guard, and the same number at a certain distance furnished the rear. The body of the detachment, fifteen strong, with the sumpter mules, generally followed Theodora, by whose side, whenever the way permitted, rode their commander. Since he left England Lothair had never been so much alone with Theodora. What struck him most now, as indeed previously at the camp, was that she never alluded to the past. For her there would seem to be no Muriel Towers, no Belmont, no England. You

would have supposed that she had been born in the
Apennines and had never quitted them. All her
conversation was details, political or military. Not
that her manner was changed to Lothair. It was
not only as kind as before, but it was sometimes
unusually and even unnecessarily tender, as if she
reproached herself for the too frequent and too
evident self-engrossment of her thoughts, and wished
to intimate to him that though her brain were absorbed, her heart was still gentle and true.

Two hours after noon they halted in a green
nook, near a beautiful cascade that descended in a
mist down a sylvan cleft, and poured its pellucid
stream, for their delightful use, into a natural basin
of marble. The men picketted their horses, and
their corporal, who was a man of the country and
their guide, distributed their rations. All vied with
each other in administering to the comfort and convenience of Theodora, and Lothair hovered about
her as a bee about a flower, but she was silent,
which he wished to impute to fatigue. But she said
she was not at all fatigued, indeed quite fresh. Before they resumed their journey he could not refrain
from observing on the beauty of their resting-place.
She assented with a pleasing nod, and then resum-
ing her accustomed abstraction she said — "The
more I think, the more I am convinced that the
battle is not to be fought in this country, but in
France."

After one more ascent, and that comparatively a
gentle one, it was evident that they were gradually
emerging from the mountainous region. Their course

since their halting lay through a spur of the chief
chain they had hitherto pursued, and a little after
sunset they arrived at a farm-house, which the corporal informed his Captain was the intended quarter
of Theodora for the night, as the horses could pro-
ceed no farther without rest. At dawn they were
to resume their way, and soon to cross the open
country, where danger, if any, was to be anticipated.

The farmer was frightened when he was summoned from his house by a party of armed men;
but having some good ducats given him in advance,
and being assured they were all Christians, he took
heart and laboured to do what they desired. Theodora duly found herself in becoming quarters, and
a sentry was mounted at her residence. The troopers,
who had been quite content to wrap themselves in
their cloaks and pass the night in the air, were
pleased to find no despicable accommodation in the
out-buildings of the farm, and still more with the
proffered vintage of their host. As for Lothair, he
enveloped himself in his mantle and threw himself
on a bed of sacks, with a truss of Indian corn for
his pillow, and though he began by musing over
Theodora, in a few minutes he was immersed in
that profound and dreamless sleep which a life of
action and mountain air combined can alone secure.

CHAPTER IX.

THE open country extending from the Apennines
to the very gates of Rome, and which they had now
to cross, was in general a desert; a plain clothed
with a coarse vegetation, and undulating with an
interminable series of low and uncouth mounds,
without any of the grace of form which always attends the disposition of nature. Nature had not
created them. They were the offspring of man and
time, and of their rival powers of destruction. Ages
of civilisation were engulfed in this drear expanse.
They were the tombs of empires and the sepulchres
of contending races. The Campagna proper has at
least the grace of aqueducts to break its monotony,
and everywhere the cerulean spell of distance; but
in this grim solitude antiquity has left only the
memory of its violence and crimes, and nothing is
beautiful except the sky.

The orders of the General to direct their course
as much as possible in the vicinity of the Italian
frontier, though it lengthened their journey, somewhat mitigated its dreariness, and an hour after
noon, after traversing some flinty fields, they observed in the distance an olive wood, beneath the
pale shade of which, and among whose twisted
branches and contorted roots, they had contemplated
finding a halting-place. But here the advanced

guard observed already an encampment, and one of them rode back to report the discovery.

A needless alarm; for after a due reconnaissance, they were ascertained to be friends—a band of patriots about to join the General in his encampment among the mountains. They reported that a division of the Italian army was assembled in force upon the frontier, but that several regiments had already signified to their commanders that they would not fight against Garibaldi or his friends. They confirmed also the news that the great leader himself was a prisoner at Caprera; that although his son Menotti by his command had withdrawn from Nerola, his force was really increased by the junction of Ghirelli and the Roman legion, twelve hundred strong, and that five hundred riflemen would join the General in the course of the week.

A little before sunset they had completed the passage of the open country, and had entered the opposite branch of the Apennines, which they had long observed in the distance. After wandering among some rocky ground, they entered a defile amid hills covered with ilex, and thence emerging found themselves in a valley of some expanse and considerable cultivation; bright crops, vineyards in which the vine was married to the elm, orchards full of fruit, and groves of olive; in the distance blue hills that were becoming dark in the twilight, and in the centre of the plain, upon a gentle and wooded elevation, a vast pile of building, the exact character of which at this hour it was difficult to recognise, for even as Theodora mentioned to Lothair that they now beheld the object of their journey the twilight seemed to vanish and the stars glistened in the dark heavens.

Though the building seemed so near, it was yet a considerable time before they reached the wooded hill, and though its ascent was easy, it was night before they halted in face of a huge gate flanked by high stone walls. A single light in one of the windows of the vast pile which it enclosed was the only evidence of human habitation.

The corporal sounded a bugle, and immediately the light moved and noises were heard—the opening of the hall doors, and then the sudden flame of torches, and the advent of many feet. The great gate slowly opened, and a steward and several serving men appeared. The steward addressed Theodora and Lothair, and invited them to dismount and enter what now appeared to be a garden with statues and terraces and fountains and rows of cypress, its infinite dilapidation not being recognisable in the deceptive hour; and he informed the escort that their quarters were prepared for them, to which they were at once attended. Guiding their Captain and his charge, they soon approached a double flight of steps, and ascending, reached the main terrace from which the building immediately rose. It was, in truth, a castle of the middle ages, on which a Roman prince, at the commencement of the last century, had engrafted the character of one of those vast and ornate villas then the mode, but its original character still asserted itself, and notwithstanding its Tuscan basement and its Ionic pilasters, its rich pediments and delicate volutes, in the distant landscape it still seemed a fortress in the commanding position which became the residence of a feudal chief.

They entered through a Palladian vestibule a hall which they felt must be of huge dimensions, though with the aid of a single torch it was impossible to trace its limits, either of extent or of elevation. Then bowing before them, and lighting as it were their immediate steps, the steward guided them down a long and lofty corridor, which led to the entrance of several chambers, all vast, with little furniture, but their walls covered with pictures. At length he opened a door and ushered them into a saloon, which was in itself bright and glowing, but of which the lively air was heightened by its contrast with the preceding scene. It was lofty, and hung with faded satin in gilded panels still bright. An ancient chandelier of Venetian crystal hung illumined from the painted ceiling, and on the silver dogs of the marble hearth a fresh block of cedar had just been thrown and blazed with aromatic light.

A lady came forward and embraced Theodora, and then greeted Lothair with cordiality. "We must dine to-day even later than you do in London," said the Princess of Tivoli, "but we have been expecting you these two hours." Then she drew Theodora aside, and said, "He is here; but you must be tired, my best beloved. As some wise man said: 'Business to-morrow.'"

"No, no," said Theodora; "now, now—I am

5*

never tired. The only thing that exhausts me is suspense."

"It shall be so. At present I will take you away
to shake the dust off your armour; and Serafino attend to Captain Muriel."

CHAPTER X.

WHEN they assembled again in the saloon there
was an addition to their party in the person of a
gentleman of distinguished appearance. His age
could hardly have much exceeded that of thirty, but
time had agitated his truly Roman countenance, one
which we now find only in consular and imperial
busts, or in the chance visage of a Roman shepherd
or a Neapolitan bandit. He was a shade above the
middle height, with a frame of well-knit symmetry.
His proud head was proudly placed on broad shoulders,
and neither time nor indulgence had marred his
slender waist. His dark brown hair was short and
hyacinthine, close to his white forehead, and naturally showing his small ears. He wore no whiskers,
and his moustache was limited to the centre of his
upper lip.

When Theodora entered and offered him her
hand he pressed it to his lips with gravity and proud
homage, and then their hostess said, "Captain Muriel,
let me present you to a Prince who will not bear his
titles, and whom, therefore, I must call by his name
—Romolo Colonna."

LOTHAIR. 69

The large folding doors, richly painted and gilt, though dim from neglect and time, and sustained by columns of precious marbles, were suddenly opened and revealed another saloon, in which was a round table brightly lighted, and to which the Princess invited her friends.

Their conversation at dinner was lively and sustained; the travels of the last two days formed a natural part and were apposite to commence with, but they were soon engrossed in the great subject of their lives; and Colonna, who had left Rome only four-and-twenty hours, gave them interesting details of the critical condition of that capital. When the repast was concluded the Princess rose, and, accompanied by Lothair, re-entered the saloon, but Theodora and Colonna lingered behind, and finally seating themselves at the farthest end of the apartment in which they had dined became engaged in earnest conversation.

"You have seen a great deal since we first met at Belmont," said the Princess to Lothair.

"It seems to me now," said Lothair, "that I knew as much of life then as I did of the stars above us, about whose purposes and fortunes I used to puzzle myself."

"And might have remained in that ignorance. The great majority of men exist but do not live—like Italy in the last century. The power of the passions, the force of the will, the creative energy of the imagination—these make life, and reveal to us a world of which the million are entirely ignorant. You have been fortunate in your youth to have be-

come acquainted with a great woman. It develops
all a man's powers, and gives him a thousand
talents."

"I often think," said Lothair, "that I have
neither powers nor talents, but am drifting without
an orbit."

"Into infinite space," said the Princess. "Well,
one might do worse than that. But it is not so. In
the long run your nature will prevail, and you will
fulfil your organic purpose; but you will accomplish
your ends with a completeness which can only be
secured by the culture and development you are now
experiencing."

"And what is my nature?" said Lothair. "I wish
you would tell me."

"Has not the divine Theodora told you?"

"She has told me many things, but not that."

"How then could I know," said the Princess,
"if she has not discovered it?"

"But perhaps she has discovered it," said Lothair.

"Oh! then she would tell you," said the Princess, "for she is the soul of truth."

"But she is also the soul of kindness, and she
might wish to spare my feelings."

"Well, that is very modest, and I dare say not
affected. For there is no man, however gifted, even
however conceited, who has any real confidence in
himself until he has acted."

"Well, we shall soon act," said Lothair, "and
then I suppose I shall know my nature."

"In time," said the Princess, "and with the continued inspiration of friendship."

"But you too are a great friend of Theodora?"

"Although a woman. I see you are laughing at female friendships, and, generally speaking, there is foundation for the general sneer. I will own, for my part, I have every female weakness, and in excess. I am vain, I am curious, I am jealous, and I am envious; but I adore Theodora. I reconcile my feelings towards her and my disposition in this way. It is not friendship—it is worship. And indeed there are moments when I sometimes think she is one of those beautiful divinities that we once worshipped in this land, and who, when they listened to our prayers, at least vouchsafed that our country should not be the terrible wilderness that you crossed this day."

In the meantime Colonna, with folded arms and eyes fixed on the ground, was listening to Theodora.

"Thus you see," she continued, "it comes to this—Rome can only be freed by the Romans. He looks upon the secret societies of his own country as he does upon universal suffrage—a wild beast, and dangerous, but which may be watched and tamed and managed by the police. He listens, but he plays with them. He temporises. At the bottom of his heart, his Italian blood despises the Gauls. It must be something deeper and more touching than this. Rome must appeal to him, and in the ineffable name."

"It has been uttered before," said Colonna, looking up at his companion, "and——" And he
hesitated.

"And in vain you would say," said Theodora.
"Not so. There was a martyrdom, but the blood of
Felice baptised the new birth of Italian life. But I
am not thinking of bloodshed. Had it not been for
the double intrigues of the Savoyards it need not
then have been shed. We bear him no ill will—at
least not now—and we can make great offers. Make
them. The revolution in Gaul is ever a mimicry of
Italian thought and life. Their great affair of the
last century, which they have so marred and muddled,
would never have occurred had it not been for Tuscan reform; 1848 was the echo of our societies; and
the Seine will never be disturbed if the Tiber flows
unruffled. Let him consent to Roman freedom, and
MADRE NATURA will guarantee him against Lutetian
barricades."

"It is only the offer of Mary-Anne in another
form," said Colonna.

"Guarantee the dynasty," said Theodora. "There
is the point. He can trust us. Emperors and kings
break treaties without remorse, but he knows that
what is registered by the most ancient power in the
world is sacred."

"Can republicans guarantee dynasties?" said Colonna, shaking his head.

"Why, what is a dynasty, when we are dealing
with eternal things? The casualties of life compared
with infinite space. Rome is eternal. Centuries of
the most degrading and foreign priestcraft—enervat-

ing rites brought in by Heliogabalus and the Syrian emperors—have failed to destroy her. Dynasties! Why, even in our dark servitude we have seen Merovingian and Carlovingian kings, and Capets and Valois and Bourbons and now Buonapartes. They have disappeared, and will disappear like Orgetorix and the dynasties of the time of Cæsar. What we want is Rome free. Do not you see that everything has been preparing for that event? This monstrous masquerade of United Italy—what is it but an initiatory ceremony to prove that Italy without Rome is a series of provinces? Establish the Roman republic, and the Roman race will, as before, conquer them in detail. And when the Italians are thus really united, what will become of the Gauls? Why, the first Buonaparte said that if Italy were really united the Gauls would have no chance. And he was a good judge of such things."

"What would you have me do then?" said Colonna.

"See him—see him at once. Say everything that I have said, and say it better. His disposition is with us. Convenience, all political propriety, counsel and would justify his abstinence. A return to Rome would seem weak, fitful, capricious, and would prove that his previous retirement was ill-considered and ill-informed. It would disturb and alarm Europe. But you have, nevertheless, to fight against great odds. It is MADRE NATURA against ST. PETER'S. Never was the abomination of the world so active as at present. It is in the very throes of its fell

despair.   To save itself, it would poison in the
Eucharist."

"And If I fail?" said Colonna.

"You will not fail. On the whole his interest
lies on our side."

"The sacerdotal influences are very strong there.
When the calculation of interest is fine, a word, a
glance, sometimes a sigh, a tear, may have a fatal
effect."

"All depends upon him," said Theodora. "If
he were to disappear from the stage, interference
would be impossible."

"But he is on the stage, and apparently will remain."

"A single life should not stand between Rome
and freedom."

"What do you mean?"

"I mean that Romolo Colonna should go to Paris
and free his country."

CHAPTER XI.

WHEN Captain Muriel and his detachment returned to the camp, they found that the force had
been not inconsiderably increased in their absence,
while the tidings of the disposition of the Italian
army, brought by the recruits and the deserters from
the royal standard, cherished the hopes of the troops,
and stimulated their desire for action. Theodora
had been far more communicative during their

journey back than in that of her departure. She
was less absorbed, and had resumed that serene yet
ever sympathising character which was one of her
charms. Without going into detail, she mentioned
more than once to Lothair how relieved she felt by
Colonna accepting the mission to Paris. He was a
person of so much influence, she said, and of such
great judgment and resource. She augured the most
satisfactory results from his presence on the main
scene of action.

Time passed rapidly at the camp. When a life
of constant activity is combined with routine, the
hours fly. Neither letter nor telegram arrived from
Colonna, and neither was expected; and yet Theodora
heard from him, and even favourably. One day, as
she was going the rounds with her husband, a young
soldier, a new recruit, approached her, and pressing
to his lips a branch of the olive tree, presented it to
her. On another occasion when she returned to her
tent, she found a bunch of fruit from the same tree,
though not quite ripe, which showed that the cause
of peace had not only progressed but had almost
matured. All these communications sustained her
sanguine disposition, and full of happy confidence
she laboured with unceasing and inspiring energy,
so that when the looked-for signal came they might
be prepared to obey it, and rapidly gather the rich
fruition of their glorious hopes.

While she was in this mood of mind a scout
arrived from Nerola, bringing news that a brigade of
the French army had positively embarked at Marseilles, and might be hourly expected at Civita Vec-

chia. The news was absolute. The Italian Consul
at Marseilles had telegraphed to his government both
when the first regiment was on board, and when the
last had embarked. Copies of these telegrams had
been forwarded instantly by a secret friend to the
volunteers on the southern frontier.

When Theodora heard this news she said nothing, but, turning pale, she quitted the group round
the General and hastened to her own tent. She told
her attendant, the daughter of the custom-house
officer at Narni, and a true child of the mountains,
that no one must approach her, not even Colonel
Campian, and the girl sate without the tent at its
entrance, dressed in her many coloured garments,
with fiery eyes and square white teeth, and her dark
hair braided with gold coins and covered with a long
white kerchief of perfect cleanliness; and she had a
poniard at her side and a revolver in her hand, and
she would have used both weapons sooner than that
her mistress should be disobeyed.

Alone in her tent, Theodora fell upon her knees,
and lifting up her hands to heaven and bowing her
head to the earth, she said: "O God! whom I have
ever worshipped, God of justice and of truth, receive
the agony of my soul!"

And on the earth she remained for hours in
despair.

Night came and it brought no solace, and the
day returned, but to her it brought no light. Theodora
was no longer seen. The soul of the camp seemed
extinct. The mien of majesty that ennobled all; the
winning smile that rewarded the rifleman at his

practice and the sapper at his toil; the inciting word that reanimated the recruit and recalled to the veteran the glories of Sicilian struggles—all vanished—all seemed spiritless and dull, and the armourer clinked his forge as if he were the heartless hireling of a king.

In this state of moral discomfiture there was one person who did not lose his head, and this was the General. Calm, collected, and critical, he surveyed the situation and indicated the possible contingencies. "Our best, if not our only, chance," he said to Colonel Campian, "is this—that the Italian army now gathered in force upon the frontier should march to Rome and arrive there before the French. Whatever then happens, we shall at least get rid of the great imposture, but in all probability the French and Italians will fight. In that case I shall join the Savoyards, and in the confusion we may do some business yet."

"This embarkation," said the Colonel, "explains the gathering of the Italians on the frontier. They must have foreseen this event at Florence. They never can submit to another French occupation. It would upset their throne. The question is, who will be at Rome first."

"Just so," said the General; "and as it is an affair upon which all depends, and is entirely beyond my control, I think I shall now take a nap." So saying he turned into his tent, and, in five minutes, this brave and exact man, but in whom the muscular development far exceeded the nervous, was slumbering without a dream.

Civita Vecchia was so near at hand, and the scouts of the General were so numerous and able, that he soon learnt the French had not yet arrived, and another day elapsed and still no news of the French. But, on the afternoon of the following day, the startling but authentic information arrived, that, after the French army having embarked and remained two days in port, the original orders had been countermanded, and the troops had absolutely disembarked.

There was a cheer in the camp when the news was known, and Theodora started from her desolation, surprised that there could be in such a scene a sound of triumph. Then there was another cheer, and though she did not move, but remained listening and leaning on her arm, the light returned to her eyes. The cheer was repeated, and there were steps about her tent. She caught the voice of Lothair speaking to her attendant, and adjuring her to tell her mistress immediately that there was good news, and that the French troops had disembarked. Then he heard her husband calling Theodora.

The camp became a scene of excitement and festivity which, in general, only succeeds some signal triumph. The troops lived always in the air, except in the hours of night, when the atmosphere of the mountains in the late autumn is dangerous. At present they formed groups and parties in the vicinity of the tents; there was their gay canteen and there their humorous kitchen. The man of the Gulf with his rich Venetian banter and the Sicilian with his scaramouch tricks got on very well with the gentle

and polished Tuscan, and could amuse without
offending the high Roman soul; but there were some
quips and cranks and sometimes some antics which
were not always relished by the simpler men from
the islands, and the offended eye of a Corsican sometimes seemed to threaten "vendetta."

About sunset, Colonel Campian led forth Theodora. She was in female attire, and her long hair
restrained only by a fillet reached nearly to the
ground. Her Olympian brow seemed distended; a
phosphoric light glittered in her Hellenic eyes; a
deep. pink spot burnt upon each of those cheeks
usually so immaculately fair.

The General and the chief officers gathered
round her with their congratulations, but she would
visit all the quarters. She spoke to the men in all
the dialects of that land of many languages. The
men of the Gulf, in general of gigantic stature,
dropped their merry Venetian stories and fell down
on their knees and kissed the hem of her garment;
the Scaramouch forgot his tricks, and wept as he
would to the Madonna; Tuscany and Rome made
speeches worthy of the Arno and the Forum; and
the Corsicans and the islanders unsheathed their
poniards and brandished them in the air, which is
their mode of denoting affectionate devotion. As
the night advanced, the crescent moon glittering
above the Apennine, Theodora attended by the
whole staff, having visited all the troops, stopped at
the chief fire of the camp, and in a voice which
might have maddened nations sang the hymn of
Roman liberty, the whole army ranged in ranks along

the valley joining in the solemn and triumphant chorus.

CHAPTER XII.

THIS exaltation of feeling in the camp did not evaporate. All felt that they were on the eve of some great event, and that the hour was at hand. And it was in this state of enthusiasm, that couriers arrived with the intelligence that Garibaldi had escaped from Caprera, that he had reached Nerola in safety, and was in command of the assembled forces; and that the General was, without loss of time, to strike his camp, join the main body at a given place, and then march to Rome.

The breaking-up of the camp was as the breaking-up of a long frost and the first scent of spring. There was a brightness in every man's face and a gay elasticity in all their movements. But when the order of the day informed them that they must prepare for instant combat, and that in eight and forty hours they would probably be in face of the enemy, the hearts of the young recruits fluttered with strange excitement, and the veterans nodded to each other with grim delight.

It was nearly midnight when the troops quitted the valley through a defile in an opposite direction to the pass by which they had entered it. It was a bright night. Colonel Campian had the command of the division in advance, which was five hundred

strong. After the defile, the country though hilly
was comparatively open, and here the advanced
guard was to halt until the artillery and cavalry had
effected the passage, and this was the most laborious
and difficult portion of the march, but all was well
considered, and all went right. The artillery and
cavalry by sunrise had joined the advanced guard
who were bivouacking in the rocky plain, and about
noon the main columns of the infantry began to de-
ploy from the heights, and in a short time the whole
force was in the field. Soon after this some of the
skirmishers who had been sent forward returned,
and reported the enemy in force and in a strong
position, commanding the intended route of the invading force. On this the General resolved to halt
for a few hours, and rest and refresh the troops, and
to recommence their march after sunset, so that,
without effort, they might be in the presence of the
enemy by dawn.

Lothair had been separated from Theodora during this to him novel and exciting scene. She had
accompanied her husband, but when the whole force
advanced in battle array, the General had desired
that she should accompany the staff. They advanced
through the night, and by dawn they were fairly in
the open country. In the distance, and in the middle
of the rough and undulating plain, was a round hill
with an ancient city, for it was a bishop's see, built
all about and over it. It would have looked like a
gigantic beehive, had it not been for a long convent
on the summit, flanked by some stone pines, as we
see in the pictures of Gaspar and Claude.

Between this city and the invading force, though
not in a direct line, was posted the enemy in a
strong position; their right wing protected by one of
the mounds common in the plain, and their left
backed by an olive wood of considerable extent, and
which grew on the last rocky spur of the mountains.
They were therefore, as regards the plain, on commanding ground.   The strength of the two forces
was not unequal, and the Papal troops were not to
be despised, consisting among others of a detachment of the legion of Antibes and the Zouaves.
They had artillery, which was well posted.

The General surveyed the scene, for which he
was not unprepared.   Disposing his troops in positions in which they were as much protected as possible from the enemy's fire, he opened upon them a
fierce and continuous cannonade, while he ordered
Colonel Campian and eight hundred men to fall
back among the hills, and following a circuitous
path, which had been revealed by a shepherd, gain
the spur of the mountains and attack the enemy in
their rear through the olive wood.   It was calculated
that this movement, if successful, would require about
three hours, and the General, for that period of the
time, had to occupy the enemy and his own troops
with what were in reality feint attacks.

When the calculated time had elapsed, the General
became anxious, and his glass was never from his
eye.   He was posted on a convenient ridge, and the
wind, which was high this day from the sea, frequently cleared the field from the volumes of smoke;
so his opportunities of observation were good.   But

the three hours passed, and there was no sign of the
approach of Campian, and he ordered Sarano with
his division to advance towards the mound and occupy the attention of the right wing of the enemy;
but very shortly after Lothair had carried this order,
and four hours having elapsed, the General observed
some confusion in the left wing of the enemy, and
instantly countermanding the order, commanded a
general attack in line. The troops charged with enthusiasm, but they were encountered with a resolution as determined. At first they carried the mound,
broke the enemy's centre, and were mixed up with
their great guns; but the enemy fiercely rallied, and
the invaders were repulsed. The Papal troops retained their position, and their opponents were in
disorder on the plain and a little dismayed. It was
at this moment that Theodora rushed forward, and
waving a sword in one hand, and in the other the
standard of the Republic, exclaimed "Brothers, to
Rome!"

This sight inflamed their faltering hearts, which
after all were rather confounded than dismayed.
They formed and rallied round her, and charged
with renewed energy at the very moment that Campian
had brought the force of his division on the enemy's
rear. A panic came over the Papal troops, thus
doubly assailed, and their rout was complete. They
retreated in the utmost disorder to Viterbo, which
they abandoned that night and hurried to Rome.

At the last moment, when the victory was no
longer doubtful, and all were in full retreat or in full
pursuit, a Zouave, in wantonness firing his weapon

before he threw it away, sent a random shot which
struck Theodora, and she fell. Lothair, who had
never left her during the battle, was at her side in
a moment, and a soldier, who had also marked the
fatal shot; and, strange to say, so hot and keen was
the pursuit, that though a moment before they seemed
to be in the very thick of the strife, they almost in-
stantaneously found themselves alone, or rather with
no companions than the wounded near them. She
looked at Lothair, but at first could not speak. She
seemed stunned, but soon murmured, "Go, go; you
are wanted."

At this moment the General rode up with some
of his staff. His countenance was elate and his eye
sparkled with fire. But catching the figure of Lothair
kneeling on the field, he reined in his charger and
said, "What is this?" Then looking more closely,
he instantly dismounted, and muttering to himself,
"This mars the victory," he was at Theodora's
side.

A slight smile came over her when she recognised
the General, and she faintly pressed his hand, and
then said again, "Go, go; you are all wanted."

"None of us are wanted. The day is won; we
must think of you."

"Is it won?" she murmured.

"Complete."

"I die content."

"Who talks of death?" said the General. "This
is a wound, but I have had some worse. What we
must think of now are remedies. I passed an ambulance this moment. Run for it," he said to his

aide-de-camp. "We must staunch the wound at once; but it is only a mile to the city, and then we shall find everything, for we were expected. I will ride on, and there shall be proper attendance ready before you arrive. You will conduct our friend to the city," he said to Lothair, "and be of good courage, as I am."

CHAPTER XIII.

THE troops were rushing through the gates of the city when the General rode up. There was a struggling and stifling crowd; cheers and shrieks. It was that moment of wild fruition, when the master is neither recognised nor obeyed. It is not easy to take a bone out of a dog's mouth; nevertheless the presence of the General in time prevailed, something like order was established, and before the ambulance could arrive, a guard had been appointed to receive it, and the ascent to the monastery, where a quarter was prepared, kept clear.

During the progress to the city Theodora never spoke, but she seemed stunned rather than suffering; and once, when Lothair, who was walking by her side, caught her glance with his sorrowful and anxious face, she put forth her hand and pressed his.

The ascent to the convent was easy, and the advantages of air and comparative tranquillity, which the place offered, counterbalanced the risk of post-

poning, for a very brief space, the examination of
the wound.

They laid her on their arrival on a large bed,
without poles or canopy, in a lofty white-washed
room of considerable dimensions, clean and airy,
with high open windows. There was no furniture
in the room except a chair, a table, and a crucifix.
Lothair took her in his arms and laid her on the
bed; and the common soldier who had hitherto assisted him, a giant in stature with a beard a foot
long, stood by the bedside crying like a child. The
chief surgeon almost at the same moment arrived
with an aide-de-camp of the General, and her faithful female attendant, and in a few minutes her husband, himself wounded and covered with dust.

The surgeon at once requested that all should
withdraw except her devoted maid, and they waited
his report without, in that deep sad silence which
will not despair, and yet dares not hope.

When the wound had been examined and probed
and dressed, Theodora in a faint voice said, "Is it
desperate?"

"Not desperate," said the surgeon, "but serious.
All depends upon your perfect tranquillity—of mind
as well as body."

"Well I am here and cannot move; and as for
my mind, I am not only serene but happy."

"Then we shall get through this," said the surgeon encouragingly.

"I do not like you to stay with me," said Theodora. "There are other sufferers besides myself."

"My orders are not to quit you," said the sur-

geon, "but I can be of great use within these walls.
I shall return when the restorative has had its effect.
But remember, if I be wanted, I am always here."

Soon after this Theodora fell into a gentle
slumber, and after two hours woke refreshed. The
countenance of the surgeon when he again visited
her was less troubled; it was hopeful.

The day was now beginning to decline; notwithstanding the scenes of tumult and violence near at
hand, all was here silent; and the breeze, which
had been strong during the whole day, but which
blew from the sea, and was very soft, played gratefully upon the pale countenance of the sufferer.
Suddenly she said, "What is that?"

And they answered and said, "We heard
nothing."

"I hear the sound of great guns," said Theodora.

And they listened, and in a moment both the
surgeon and the maid heard the sound of distant
ordnance.

"The Liberator is at hand," said the maid.

"I dare say," said the surgeon.

"No;" said Theodora looking distressed. "The
sounds do not come from his direction. Go and
see, Dolores; ask and tell me what are these
sounds."

The surgeon was sitting by her side, and occasionally touching her pulse, or wiping the slight
foam from her brow, when Dolores returned and
said, "Lady, the sounds are the great guns of Civita
Vecchia."

A deadly change came over the countenance of

Theodora, and the surgeon looked alarmed. He would have given her some restorative, but she refused it. "No, kind friend," she said; "it is finished. I have just received a wound more fatal than the shot in the field this morning. The French are at Rome. Tell me, kind friend, how long do you think I may live?"

The surgeon felt her pulse; his look was gloomy. "In such a case as yours," he said, "the patient is the best judge."

"I understand," she said. "Send then at once for my husband."

He was at hand, for his wound had been dressed in the convent, and he came to Theodora with his arm in a sling, but with the attempt of a cheerful visage.

In the meantime, Lothair, after having heard the first, and by no means hopeless, bulletin of the surgeon, had been obliged to leave the convent to look after his men, and having seen them in quarters and made his report to the General, he obtained permission to return to the convent and ascertain the condition of Theodora. Arrived there, he heard that she had had refreshing slumber, and that her husband was now with her, and a ray of hope lighted up the darkness of his soul. He was walking up and down the refectory of the convent with that sickening restlessness which attends impending and yet uncertain sorrow, when Colonel Campian entered the apartment and beckoned to him.

There was an expression in his face which appalled Lothair, and he was about to enquire after

Theodora, when his tongue cleaved to the roof of his mouth and he could not speak. The Colonel shook his head, and said in a low, hollow voice, "She wishes to see you, and alone. Come."

Theodora was sitting in the bed propped up by cushions when Lothair entered, and as her wound was internal, there was no evidence of her sufferings. The distressful expression of her face when she heard the great guns of Civita Vecchia had passed away. It was serious, but it was serene. She bade her maid leave the chamber, and then she said to Lothair, "It is the last time I shall speak to you, and I wish that we should be alone. There is something much on my mind at this moment, and you can relieve it."

"Adored being," murmured Lothair with streaming eyes, "there is no wish of yours that I will not fulfil."

"I know your life, for you have told it me, and you are true. I know your nature; it is gentle and brave, but perhaps too susceptible. I wished it to be susceptible only of the great and good. Mark me—I have a vague but strong conviction that there will be another, and a more powerful, attempt to gain you to the Church of Rome. If I have ever been to you, as you have sometimes said, an object of kind thoughts,—if not a fortunate, at least a faithful, friend,—promise me now, at this hour of trial, with all the solemnity that becomes the moment, that you will never enter that communion."

Lothair would have spoken, but his voice was

choked, and he could only press her hand and bow his head.

"But promise me," said Theodora.

"I promise," said Lothair.

"And now," she said, "embrace me, for I wish that your spirit should be upon me as mine departs."

CHAPTER XIV.

IT was a November day in Rome, and the sky was as gloomy as the heaven of London. The wind moaned through the silent streets, deserted except by soldiers. The shops were shut, not a civilian or a priest could be seen. The Corso was occupied by the Swiss Guard and Zouaves, with artillery ready to sweep it at a moment's notice. Six of the city gates were shut and barricaded with barrels full of earth. Troops and artillery were also posted in several of the principal piazzas, and on some commanding heights, and St. Peter's itself was garrisoned.

And yet these were the arrangements rather of panic than precaution. The utmost dismay pervaded the council-chamber of the Vatican. Since the news had arrived of the disembarkation of the French troops at Marseilles, all hope of interference had expired. It was clear that Berwick had been ultimately foiled, and his daring spirit and teeming device were the last hope, as they were the ablest representation, of Roman audacity and stratagem. The Revolutionary Committee, whose abiding-place or agents never could be traced or discovered, had posted every part of the city during the night with their manifesto, announcing that the hour had arrived; an attempt, partially successful, had been made to blow up the barracks of the Zouaves; and the Cardinal Secretary was in possession of information that an insurrection was immediate, and that the city would be fired in four different quarters.

The Pope had escaped from the Vatican to the Castle of St. Angelo, where he was secure, and where his courage could be sustained by the presence of the Noble Guard with their swords always drawn. The six score of Monsignori, who in their different offices form, what is styled, the Court of Rome, had either accompanied his Holiness, or prudently secreted themselves in the strongest palaces and convents at their command. Later in the day news arrived of the escape of Garibaldi from Caprera; he was said to be marching on the city, and only five and twenty miles distant. There appeared another proclamation from the Revolutionary Committee, mysteriously posted under the very noses of the guards and police, postponing the insurrection till the arrival of the Liberator.

The Papal cause seemed hopeless. There was a general feeling throughout the city and all classes, that this time it was to be an affair of Alaric or Genseric, or the Constable of Bourbon; no negotiations, no compromises, no conventions, but slaughter, havoc, a great judicial devastation, that was to extirpate all signs and memories of Mediæval and Semitic Rome, and restore and renovate the inheritance of the true offspring of the she-wolf. The very aspect of the place itself was sinister. Whether it were the dulness of the dark sky, or the frown of MADRE NATURA herself, but the old Seven Hills seemed to look askance. The haughty Capitol, impatient of its chapels, sighed once more for triumphs; and the proud Palatine, remembering the Cæsars, glanced with imperial contempt on the palaces of the Papal princelings that, in the course of ignominious ages, had been constructed out of the exhaustless womb of its still sovereign ruin. The Jews in their quarter spoke nothing, but exchanged a curious glance, as if to say, "Has it come at last? And will they indeed serve her as she served Sion?"

This dreadful day at last passed, followed by as dreadful a night, and then another day equally gloomy, equally silent, equally panicstricken. Even insurrection would have been a relief amid the horrible and wearing suspense. On the third day the Government made some wild arrests of the wrong persons, and then came out a fresh proclamation from the Revolutionary Committee, directing the Romans to make no move until the advanced guard of Garibaldi had appeared upon Monte Mario. About this time the routed troops of the Pope arrived in confusion from Viterbo, and of course extenuated their discomfiture by exaggerating the strength of their opponents. According to them they had encountered not less than ten thousand men, who now having joined the still greater force of Garibaldi, were in full march on the city.

The members of the Papal party who showed the greatest spirit and the highest courage at this trying conjuncture, were the Roman ladies and their foreign friends. They scraped lint for the troops as incessantly as they offered prayers to the Virgin. Some of them were trained nurses, and they were training others to tend the sick and wounded. They organised a hospital service, and when the wounded arrived from Viterbo, notwithstanding the rumours of incendiarism and massacre, they came forth from their homes, and proceeded in companies, with no male attendants but armed men, to the discharge of their self-appointed public duties. There were many foreigners in the Papal ranks, and the sympathies and services of the female visitors to Rome were engaged for their countrymen. Princesses of France and Flanders might be seen by the tressel beds of many a suffering soldier of Dauphiné and Brabant; but there were numerous subjects of Queen Victoria in the Papal ranks—some Englishmen, several Scotchmen, many Irish. For them the English ladies had organised a special service. Lady St. Jerome, with unflagging zeal, presided over this department; and the superior of the sisterhood of mercy, that shrank from no toil, and feared no danger in the fulfilment of those sacred duties of pious patriots, was Miss Arundel.

She was leaning over the bed of one who had been cut down in the olive wood by a sabre of Campian's force, when a peal of artillery was heard.

She thought that her hour had arrived, and the assault had commenced.

"Most holy Mary!" she exclaimed, "sustain me."

There was another peal, and it was repeated, and again and again at regular intervals.

"That is not a battle, it is a salute," murmured the wounded soldier.

And he was right; it was the voice of the great guns telling that the French had arrived.

The consternation of the Revolutionary Committee, no longer sustained by Colonna, absent in France, was complete. Had the advanced guard of Garibaldi been in sight, it might still have been the wisest course to rise; but Monte Mario was not yet peopled by them, and an insurrection against the Papal troops, reanimated by the reported arrival of the French, and increased in numbers by the fugitives from Viterbo, would have been certainly a rash and probably a hopeless effort. And so, in the midst of confused and hesitating councils, the first division of the French force arrived at the gates of Rome, and marched into the gloomy and silent city.

Since the interference of St. Peter and St. Paul against Alaric, the Papacy had never experienced a more miraculous interposition in its favour. Shortly after this the wind changed, and the sky became serene; a sunbeam played on the flashing cross of St. Peter's; the Pope left the Castle of Angelo, and returned to the Quirinal; the Noble Guard sheathed their puissant blades; the six score of Monsignori reappeared in all their busy haunts and stately offices; and the Court of Rome, no longer despairing of the Republic, and with a spirit worthy of the Senate after Cannæ, ordered the whole of its forces into the field to combat its invaders, with the prudent addition, in order to ensure a triumph, of a brigade of French infantry armed with chassepots.

Garibaldi, who was really at hand, hearing of these events, fell back on Monte Rotondo, about fifteen miles from the city, and took up a strong position. He was soon attacked by his opponents, and defeated with considerable slaughter, and forced to fly. The Papal troops returned to Rome in triumph, but with many wounded. The Roman ladies and their friends resumed their noble duties with enthusiasm. The ambulances were apportioned to the different hospitals, and the services of all were required. Our own countrymen had suffered severely, but the skill and energy and gentle care of Clare Arundel and her companions only increased with the greater calls upon their beautiful and sublime virtue.

A woman came to Miss Arundel and told her that, in one of the ambulances, was a young man whom they could not make out. He was severely wounded, and had now swooned; but they had reason to believe he was an Englishman. Would she see him and speak to him? And she went.

The person who had summoned her was a woman of much beauty, not an uncommon quality in Rome, and of some majesty of mien, as little rare in that city. She was said, at the time when some enquiry

was made, to be Maria Serafina de Angelis, the wife
of a tailor in the Ripetta.

The ambulance was in the courtyard of the
hospital of the Santissima Trinita di Pellegrini. The
woman pointed to it, and then went away. There
was only one person in the ambulance; the rest had
been taken into the hospital, but he had been left
because he was in a swoon, and they were trying to
restore him. Those around the ambulance made
room for Miss Arundel as she approached, and she
beheld a young man, covered with the stains of
battle, and severely wounded; but his countenance
was uninjured though insensible. His eyes were
closed, and his auburn hair fell in clusters on his
white forehead. The sister of mercy touched the
pulse to ascertain whether there yet was life, but, in
the very act, her own frame became agitated, and
the colour left her cheek, as she recognised—LOTHAIR.

CHAPTER XV.

WHEN Lothair in some degree regained consciousness, he found himself in bed. The chamber was
lofty and dim, and had once been splendid. Thought-
fulness had invested it with an air of comfort rare
under Italian roofs. The fagots sparkled on the
hearth, the light from the windows was veiled with
hangings, and the draughts from the tall doors
guarded against by screens. And by his bedside
there were beautiful flowers, and a crucifix, and a
silver bell.

Where was he? He looked up at the velvet canopy above, and then at the pictures that covered the walls, but there was no familiar aspect. He remembered nothing since he was shot down in the field of Mentana, and even that incoherently.

And there had been another battle before that, followed by a catastrophe still more dreadful. When had all this happened, and where? He tried to move his bandaged form, but he had no strength, and his mind seemed weaker than his frame. But he was soon sensible that he was not alone. A veiled figure gently lifted him, and another one refreshed his pillows. He spoke, or tried to speak, but one of them pressed her finger to her shrouded lips, and he willingly relapsed into the silence which he had hardly strength enough to break.

And sometimes these veiled and gliding ministers brought him sustenance and sometimes remedies, and he complied with all their suggestions, but with absolute listlessness; and sometimes a coarser hand interposed, and sometimes he caught a countenance that was not concealed, but was ever strange. He had a vague impression that they examined and dressed his wounds, and arranged his bandages; but whether he really had wounds, and whether he were or were not bandaged, he hardly knew, and did not care to know. He was not capable of thought, and memory was an effort under which he always broke down. Day after day he remained silent and almost motionless alike in mind and body. He had a vague feeling that, after some great sorrows, and some great trials, he was in stillness and in safety; and he had an indefinite mysterious sentiment of gratitude to some unknown power, that had cherished him in his dark calamities, and poured balm and oil into his wounds.

It was in this mood of apathy that, one evening, there broke upon his ear low but beautiful voices performing the evening service of the Church. His eye glistened, his heart was touched by the vesper spell. He listened with rapt attention to the sweet and sacred strains, and when they died away he felt depressed. Would they ever sound again?

Sooner than he could have hoped, for, when he woke in the morning from his slumbers, which, strange to say, were always disturbed, for the mind and the memory seemed to work at night though in fearful and exhausting chaos, the same divine melodies that had soothed him in the eve, now sounded in the glad and grateful worship of matin praise.

"I have heard the voice of angels," he murmured to his veiled attendant.

The vesper and the matin hours became at once the epochs of his day. He was ever thinking of them, and soon was thinking of the feelings which their beautiful services celebrate and express. His mind seemed no longer altogether a blank, and the religious sentiment was the first that returned to his exhausted heart.

"There will be a requiem to-day," whispered one of his veiled attendants.

A requiem! a service for the dead; a prayer for their peace and rest! And who was dead? The bright,

the matchless one, the spell and fascination of his
life! Was it possible? Could she be dead, who
seemed vitality in its consummate form? Was there
ever such a being as Theodora? And if there were
no Theodora on earth, why should one think of
anything but heaven?

The sounds came floating down the chamber till
they seemed to cluster round his brain; sometimes
solemn, sometimes thrilling, sometimes the divine
pathos melting the human heart with celestial sympathy and heavenly solace. The tears fell fast from
his agitated vision, and he sank back exhausted,
almost insensible, on his pillow.

"The Church has a heart for all our joys and
all our sorrows, and for all our hopes, and all our
fears," whispered a veiled attendant, as she bathed
his temples with fragrant waters.

Though the condition of Lothair had at first
seemed desperate, his youthful and vigorous frame
had enabled him to rally, and with time and the infinite solicitude which he received, his case was not
without hope. But though his physical cure was
somewhat advanced, the prostration of his mind
seemed susceptible of no relief. The services of the
Church accorded with his depressed condition; they
were the only events of his life, and he cherished
them. His attendants now permitted and even encouraged him to speak, but he seemed entirely in-
curious and indifferent. Sometimes they read to
him, and he listened, but he never made remarks.
The works which they selected had a religious or
ecclesiastical bias, even while they were imaginative;

and it seemed difficult not to be interested by the ingenious fancy by which it was worked out, that everything that was true and sacred in heaven had its symbol and significance in the qualities and accidents of earth.

After a month passed in this manner, the surgeons having announced that Lothair might now prepare to rise from his bed, a veiled attendant said to him one day, "There is a gentleman here who is a friend of yours, and who would like to see you. And perhaps you would like to see him also for other reasons, for you must have much to say to God after all that you have suffered. And he is a most holy man."

"I have no wish to see anyone. Are you sure he is not a stranger?" asked Lothair.

"He is in the next room," said the attendant. "He has been here throughout your illness, conducting our services; often by your bedside when you were asleep, and always praying for you."

The veiled attendant drew back and waved her hand, and some one glided forward and said in a low, soft voice, "You have not forgotten me?"

And Lothair beheld Monsignore Catesby.

"It is a long time since we met," said Lothair, looking at him with some scrutiny, and then all interest died away, and he turned away his vague and wandering eyes.

"But you know me?"

"I know not where I am, and I but faintly comprehend what has happened," murmured Lothair.

"You are among friends," said the Monsignore, in tones of sympathy.

"What has happened," he added, with an air of mystery, not unmixed with a certain expression of ecstasy in his glance, "must be reserved for other times, when you are stronger, and can grapple with such high themes."

"How long have I been here?" enquired Lothair, dreamingly.

"It is a month since the Annunciation."

"What Annunciation?"

"Hush!" said the Monsignore, and he raised his finger to his lip. "We must not talk of these things —at least at present. No doubt the same blessed person that saved you from the jaws of death is at this moment guarding over your recovery and guiding it; but we do not deserve, nor does the Church expect, perpetual miracles. We must avail ourselves, under Divine sanction, of the beneficent tendencies of nature; and in your case her operations must not be disturbed at this moment by any excitement, except, indeed, the glow of gratitude for celestial aid, and the inward joy which must permeate the being of anyone who feels that he is among the most favoured of men."

From this time Monsignore Catesby scarcely ever quitted Lothair. He hailed Lothair in the morn, and parted from him at night with a blessing; and in the interval Catesby devoted his whole life, and the inexhaustible resources of his fine and skilled intelligence to alleviate or amuse the existence of nis companion. Sometimes he conversed with Lothair, adroitly taking the chief burthen of the talk; and yet, whether it were bright narrative or lively disser-

tation, never seeming to lecture or hold forth, but
relieving the monologue when expedient by an interesting enquiry, which he was always ready in due
time to answer himself, or softening the instruction
by the playfulness of his mind and manner.   Sometimes he read to Lothair, and attuned the mind of
his charge to the true spiritual note by melting pas-
sages from A Kempis or Chrysostom.   Then he
would bring a portfolio of wondrous drawings by
the mediæval masters, of saints and seraphs, and
accustom the eye and thought of Lothair to the
forms and fancies of the Court of Heaven.

One day Lothair, having risen from his bed for
the first time, and lying on a sofa in an adjoining
chamber to that in which he had been so long confined, the Monsignore seated himself by the side of
Lothair, and, opening a portfolio, took out a drawing and held it before Lothair, observing his countenance with a glance of peculiar scrutiny.

"Well!" said Catesby after some little pause, as
if awaiting a remark from his companion.

"'Tis beautiful!" said Lothair.   "Is it by Raffaelle?"

"No; by Fra Bartolomeo. But the countenance,
do you remember ever having met such an one?"

Lothair shook his head. Catesby took out another drawing, the same subject, the Blessed Virgin.
"By Giulio," said the Monsignore, and he watched
the face of Lothair, but it was listless.

Then he showed Lothair another and another
and another. At last he held before him one which
was really by Raffaelle, and by which Lothair was

evidently much moved. His eye lit up, a blush suffused his pale cheek, he took the drawing himself and held it before his gaze with a trembling hand.

"Yes, I remember this," he murmured, for it was one of those faces of Greek beauty which the great painter not infrequently caught up at Rome. The Monsignore looked gently round and waved his hand, and immediately there arose the hymn to the Virgin in subdued strains of exquisite melody.

On the next morning, when Lothair woke, he found on the table by his side the drawing of the Virgin in a sliding frame.

About this time the Monsignore began to accustom Lothair to leave his apartment, and as he was not yet permitted to walk, Catesby introduced what he called an English chair, in which Lothair was enabled to survey a little the place which had been to him a refuge and a home. It seemed a building of vast size, raised round an inner court with arcades and windows, and, in the higher story where he resided, an apparently endless number of chambers and galleries. One morning, in their perambulations, the Monsignore unlocked the door of a covered way which had no light but from a lamp which guided their passage. The opposite door at the end of this covered way opened into a church, but one of a character different from any which Lothair had yet entered.

It had been raised during the latter half of the sixteenth century by Vignola, when, under the influence of the great Pagan revival, the Christian Church began to assume the character of an Olym-

pian temple. A central painted cupola of large but
exquisite proportions, supported by pilasters with
gilded capitals, and angels of white marble springing
from golden brackets; walls encrusted with rare materials of every tint, and altars supported by serpen-
tine columns of agate and alabaster; a blaze of pictures, and statues, and precious stones, and precious
metals, denoted one of the chief temples of the sacred brotherhood of Jesus, raised when the great
order had recognised that the views of primitive and
mediæval Christianity, founded on the humility of
man, were not in accordance with the age of confidence in human energy, in which they were destined to rise, and which they were determined to
direct.

Guided by Catesby, and leaning on a staff, Lothair gained a gorgeous side chapel in which mass
was celebrating; the air was rich with incense, and
all heaven seemed to open in the ministrations of a
seraphic choir. Crushed by his great calamities, both
physical and moral, Lothair sometimes felt that he
could now be content if the rest of his life could
flow away amid this celestial fragrance and these
gushing sounds of heavenly melody. And absorbed
in these feelings it was not immediately observed by
him that on the altar, behind the dazzling blaze of
tapers, was a picture of the Virgin, and identically
the same countenance as that he had recognised
with emotion in the drawing of Raffaelle.

It revived perplexing memories which agitated
him, thoughts on which it seemed his brain had not
now strength enough to dwell, and yet with which

it now seemed inevitable for him to grapple. The congregation was not very numerous, and when it broke up, several of them lingered behind and whispered to the Monsignore, and then, after a little time, Catesby approached Lothair and said, "There are some here who would wish to kiss your hand, or even touch the hem of your garments. It is troublesome, but natural, considering all that has occurred and that this is the first time, perhaps, that they may have met any one who has been so favoured."

"Favoured!" said Lothair; "am I favoured? It seems to me I am the most forlorn of men—if even I am that."

"Hush!" said the Monsignore, "we must not talk of these things at present;" and he motioned to some who approached and contemplated Lothair with blended curiosity and reverence.

These visits of Lothair to the beautiful church of the Jesuits became of daily occurrence, and often happened several times on the same day; indeed they formed the only incident which seemed to break his listlessness. He became interested in the change and variety of the services, in the persons and characters of the officiating priests. The soft manners of these fathers, their intelligence in the performance of their offices, their obliging carriage, and the unaffected concern with which all he said or did seemed to inspire them, won upon him unconsciously. The church had become his world; and his sympathies, if he still had sympathies, seemed confined to those within its walls.

In the meantime his physical advancement though slow was gradual, and had hitherto never been arrested. He could even walk a little alone, though artificially supported, and rambled about the halls and galleries full of a prodigious quantity of pictures, from the days of Raffael Sanzio to those of Raffael Mengs.

"The doctors think now we might try a little drive," said the Monsignore one morning. "The rains have ceased and refreshed everything. To-day is like the burst of spring," and when Lothair seemed to shudder at the idea of facing anything like the external world, the Monsignore suggested immediately that they should go out in a close carriage, which they finally entered in the huge quadrangle of the building. Lothair was so nervous that he pulled down even the blind of his window; and the Monsignore, who always humoured him, half pulled down his own.

Their progress seemed through a silent land and they could hardly be traversing streets. Then the ascent became a little precipitous, and then the carriage stopped and the Monsignore said, "Here is a solitary spot. We shall meet no one. The view is charming, and the air is soft." And he placed his hand gently on the arm of Lothair, and, as it were, drew him out of the carriage.

The sun was bright, and the sky was bland. There was something in the breath of nature that was delightful. The scent of violets was worth all the incense in the world; all the splendid marbles and priestly vestments seemed hard and cold when compared with the glorious colours of the cactus and the wild forms of the golden and gigantic aloes. The Favonian breeze played on the brow of this beautiful hill, and the exquisite palm trees, while they bowed their rustling heads, answered in responsive chorus to the antiphon of nature.

The dreary look that had been so long imprinted on the face of Lothair melted away.

" 'Tis well that we came, is it not?" said Catesby; "and now we will seat ourselves." Below and before them, on an undulating site, a city of palaces and churches spread out its august form, enclosing within its ample walls sometimes a wilderness of classic ruins—column and arch and theatre—sometimes the umbrageous spread of princely gardens. A winding and turbid river divided the city in unequal parts, in one of which there rose a vast and glorious temple, crowned with a dome of almost superhuman size and skill, on which the favourite sign of heaven flashed with triumphant truth.

The expression of relief which, for a moment, had reposed on the face of Lothair, left it when he said in an agitated voice, "I at length behold Rome!"

CHAPTER XVI

THE recognition of Rome by Lothair evinced not only a consciousness of locality, but an interest in it not before exhibited; and the Monsignore soon after seized the opportunity of drawing the mind of his companion to the past, and feeling how far he now realised the occurrences that immediately preceded his arrival in the city. But Lothair would not dwell on them. "I wish to think of nothing," he said, "that happened before I entered this city: all I desire now is to know those to whom I am indebted for my preservation in a condition that seemed hopeless."

"There is nothing hopeless with Divine aid," said the Monsignore; "but, humanly speaking, you are indebted for your preservation to English friends, long and intimately cherished. It is under their roof that you dwell, the Agostini palace, tenanted by Lord St. Jerome."

"Lord St. Jerome!" murmured Lothair to himself.

"And the ladies of his house are those who, only with some slight assistance from my poor self, tended you throughout your most desperate state, and when we sometimes almost feared that mind and body were alike wrecked."

"I have a dream of angels," said Lothair; "and

sometimes I listened to heavenly voices that I seemed to have heard before."

"I am sure you have not forgotten the ladies of that house?" said Catesby watching his countenance.

"No; one of them summoned me to meet her at Rome," murmured Lothair, "and I am here."

"That summons was divine," said Catesby, "and only the herald of the great event that was ordained and has since occurred. In this holy city, Miss Arundel must ever count as the most sanctified of her sex."

Lothair relapsed into silence, which subsequently appeared to be meditation, for when the carriage stopped, and the Monsignore assisted him to alight, he said, "I must see Lord St. Jerome."

And in the afternoon, with due and preparatory announcement, Lord St. Jerome waited on Lothair. The Monsignore ushered him into the chamber, and, though he left them as it were alone, never quitted it. He watched them conversing, while he seemed to be arranging books and flowers; he hovered over the conference, dropping down on them at a critical moment, when the words became either languid or embarrassing. Lord St. Jerome was a hearty man, simple and high-bred. He addressed Lothair with all his former kindness, but with some degree of reserve, and even a dash of ceremony. Lothair was not insensible to the alteration in his manner, but could ascribe it to many causes. He was himself resolved to make an effort, when Lord St. Jerome rose to depart, and expressed the intention of Lady

St. Jerome to wait on him on the morrow. "No, my dear Lord," said Lothair; "to-morrow I make my first visit, and it shall be to my best friends. I would try to come this evening, but they will not be alone; and I must see them alone, if it be only once."

This visit of the morrow rather pressed on the nervous system of Lothair. It was no slight enterprise, and called up many recollections. He brooded over his engagement during the whole evening, and his night was disturbed. His memory, long in a state of apathy, or curbed and controlled into indifference, seemed endowed with unnatural vitality, reproducing the history of his past life in rapid and exhausting tumult. All its scenes rose before him— Brentham, and Vauxe, and Muriel—and closing with one absorbing spot, which, for a long time, it avoided, and in which all merged and ended— Belmont. Then came that anguish of the heart, which none can feel but those who in the youth of life have lost some one infinitely fascinating and dear, and the wild query why he too had not fallen on the fatal plain which had entombed all the hope and inspiration of his existence.

The interview was not so trying an incident as Lothair anticipated, as often under such circumstances occurs. Miss Arundel was not present; and in the second place, although Lothair could not at first be insensible to a change in the manner of Lady St. Jerome, as well as in that of her lord, exhibiting as it did a degree of deference and ceremony which with her towards him were quite unusual, still the genial, gushing nature of this lively and enthusiastic woman, full of sympathy, soon asserted itself, and her heart was overflowing with sorrow for all his sufferings, and gratitude for his escape.

"And after all," she said, "everything must have been ordained; and, without these trials and even calamities, that great event could not have been brought about which must make all hail you as the most favoured of men."

Lothair stared with a look of perplexity and then said, "If I be the most favoured of men, it is only because two angelic beings have deigned to minister to me in my sorrow, with a sweet devotion I can never forget, and, alas! can never repay."

CHAPTER XVII.

LOTHAIR was not destined to meet Clare Arundel alone or only in the presence of her family. He had acceded, after a short time, to the wish of Lady St. Jerome, and the advice of Monsignore Catesby, to wait on her in the evening, when Lady St. Jerome was always at home and never alone. Her rooms were the privileged resort of the very cream of Roman society and of those English who, like herself, had returned to the Roman Church. An Italian palace supplied an excellent occasion for the display of the peculiar genius of our countrywomen to make a place habitable. Beautiful carpets, baskets of

flowers, and cases of ferns, and chairs which you
could sit upon, tables covered with an infinity of
toys,—sparkling, useful, and fantastic,—huge silken
screens of rich colour, and a profusion of light, produced a scene of combined comfort and brilliancy
which made every one social who entered it, and
seemed to give a bright and graceful turn even to
the careless remarks of ordinary gossip.

Lady St. Jerome rose the moment her eye caught
the entry of Lothair, and, advancing, received him
with an air of ceremony mixed, however, with an
expression of personal devotion which was distressing to him, and singularly contrasted with the easy
and genial receptions that he remembered at Vauxe.
Then Lady St. Jerome led Lothair to her companion
whom she had just quitted, and presented him to
the Princess Tarpeia-Cinque Cento, a dame in whose
veins, it was said, flowed both consular and pontifical blood of the rarest tint.

The Princess Tarpeia-Cinque Cento was the
greatest lady in Rome; had still vast possessions—
palaces and villas and vineyards and broad farms.
Notwithstanding all that had occurred, she still
looked upon the kings and emperors of the world
as the mere servants of the Pope, and on the old
Roman nobility as still the Conscript Fathers of the
world. Her other characteristic was superstition. So
she was most distinguished by an irrepressible
haughtiness and an illimitable credulity. The only
softening circumstance was that, being in the hands
of the Jesuits, her religion did not assume an ascetic
or gloomy character. She was fond of society, and

liked to show her wondrous jewels, which were still
unrivalled, although she had presented His Holiness
in his troubles with a tiara of diamonds.

There were rumours that the Princess Tarpeia-
Cinque Cento had on occasions treated even the
highest nobility of England with a certain indifference; and all agreed that to laymen, however distinguished, her Highness was not prone too easily to
relax. But, in the present instance, it is difficult to
convey a due conception of the graciousness of her
demeanour when Lothair bent before her. She
appeared even agitated, almost rose from her seat,
·and blushed through her rouge. Lady St. Jerome,
guiding Lothair into her vacant seat, walked away.

"We shall never forget what you have done for
us," said the Princess to Lothair.

"I have done nothing," said Lothair, with a surprised air.

"Ah, that is so like gifted beings like you,"
said the Princess. "They never will think they
have done anything, even were they to save the
world."

"You are too gracious, Princess," said Lothair;
"I have no claims to esteem which all must so
value."

"Who has, if you have not?" rejoined the Princess. "Yes, it is to you and to you alone that we
must look. I am very impartial in what I say, for,
to be frank, I have not been of those who believed
that the great champion would rise without the
patrimony of St. Peter. I am ashamed to say that
I have even looked with jealousy on the energy that

has been shown by individuals in other countries;
but I now confess that I was in error. I cannot resist this manifestation. It is a privilege to have
lived when it happened. All that we can do now is
to cherish your favoured life."

"You are too kind, Madam," murmured the perplexed Lothair.

"I have done nothing," rejoined the Princess,
"and am ashamed that I have done nothing. But
it is well for you, at this season, to be at Rome; and
you cannot be better, I am sure, than under this
roof. But when the spring breaks, I hope you will
honour me, by accepting for your use a villa which
I have at Albano, and which at that season has many
charms."

There were other Roman ladies in the room only
inferior in rank and importance to the Princess
Tarpeia-Cinque Cento; and in the course of the
evening, at their earnest request, they were made
acquainted with Lothair, for it cannot be said he
was presented to them. These ladies, generally so
calm, would not wait for the ordinary ceremony of
life, but, as he approached to be introduced, sank
to the ground with the obeisance offered only to
royalty.

There were some cardinals in the apartment and
several monsignori. Catesby was there in close attendance on a pretty English countess who had just
"gone over." Her husband had been at first very
much distressed at the event, and tore himself from
the severe duties of the House of Lords in the hope
that he might yet arrive in time at Rome to save her

soul. But he was too late; and, strange to say, being of a domestic turn, and disliking family dissensions, he remained at Rome during the rest of the session, and finally "went over" himself.

Later in the evening arrived his Eminence Cardinal Berwick, for our friend had gained and bravely gained the great object of a churchman's ambition, and which even our Laud was thinking at one time of accepting, although he was to remain a firm Anglican. In the death-struggle between the Church and the Secret Societies, Berwick had been the victor, and no one in the Sacred College more truly deserved the scarlet hat.

His Eminence had a reverence of radiant devotion for the Princess Tarpeia-Cinque Cento, a glance of friendship for Lady St. Jerome, for all a courtly and benignant smile; but when he recognised Lothair, he started forward, seized and retained his hand, and then seemed speechless with emotion. "Ah! comrade in the great struggle," he at length exclaimed; "this is indeed a pleasure, and to see you here!"

Early in the evening, while Lothair was sitting by the side of the Princess, his eye had wandered round the room, not unsuccessfully, in search of Miss Arundel; and when he was free he would immediately have approached her, but she was in conversation with a Roman prince. Then when she was for a moment free, he was himself engaged; and at last he had to quit abruptly a cardinal of taste, who was describing to him a statue just discovered in the

8*

baths of Diocletian, in order to seize the occasion that again offered itself.

Her manner was constrained when he addressed her, but she gave him her hand which he pressed to his lips. Looking deeply into her violet eyes he said, "You summoned me to meet you at Rome; I am here."

"And I summoned you to other things," she answered, at first with hesitation and a blush; but then, as if rallying herself to the performance of a duty too high to allow of personal embarrassment, she added, "all of which you will perform, as becomes one favoured by Heaven."

"I have been favoured by you," said Lothair, speaking low and hurriedly; "to whom I owe my life and more than my life. Yes," he continued, "this is not the scene I would have chosen to express my gratitude to you for all that you have done for me, and my admiration of your sublime virtues; but I can no longer repress the feelings of my heart, though their utterance be as inadequate as your deeds have been transcendent."

"I was but the instrument of a higher Power."

"We are all instruments of a higher Power, but the instruments chosen are always choice."

"Ay! there it is, " said Miss Arundel; "and that is what I rejoice you feel. For it is impossible that such a selection could have been made, as in your case, without your being reserved for great results."

"I am but a shattered actor for great results," said Lothair, shaking his head.

"You have had trials," said Miss Arundel; "so had St. Ignatius, so had St. Francis, and great temptations; but these are the tests of character, of will, of spiritual power—the fine gold is searched. All things that have happened have tended and been ordained to one end, and that was to make you the champion of the Church of which you are now more than the child."

"More than the child?"

"Indeed I think so. However, this is hardly the place and occasion to dwell on such matters; and, indeed, I know your friends—my friends equally—are desirous that your convalescence should not be unnecessarily disturbed by what must be, however delightful, still agitating, thoughts; but you touched yourself unexpectedly on the theme, and at any rate you will pardon one who has the inconvenient quality of having only one thought."

"Whatever you say or think must always interest me."

"You are kind to say so. I suppose you know that our Cardinal, Cardinal Grandison, will be here in a few days?"

CHAPTER XVIII.

ALTHOUGH the reception of Lothair by his old friends and by the leaders of the Roman world was in the highest degree flattering, there was something in its tone which was perplexing to him and ambiguous. Could they be ignorant of his Italian antecedents? Impossible. Miss Arundel had admitted, or rather declared, that he had experienced great trials, and even temptations. She could only allude to what had occurred since their parting in England. But all this was now looked upon as satisfactory, because it was ordained, and tended to one end; and what was that end? His devotion to the Church of Rome, of which they admitted he was not formally a child.

It was true that his chief companion was a priest, and that he passed a great portion of his life within the walls of a church. But the priest was his familiar friend in England, who in a foreign land had nursed him with devotion in a desperate illness; and although in the great calamities, physical and moral, that had overwhelmed him, he had found solace in the beautiful services of a religion which he respected, no one for a moment had taken advantage of this mood of his suffering and enfeebled mind to entrap him into controversy, or to betray him into admissions that he might afterwards consider precipitate and immature. Indeed nothing could be more delicate than the conduct of the Jesuit fathers throughout his communications with them. They seemed sincerely gratified that a suffering fellow-creature should find even temporary consolation within their fair and consecrated structure; their voices modulated with sympathy; their glances gushed with fraternal affection; their affectionate politeness contrived, in a thousand slight instances, the selection of a mass, the arrangement of a picture, the loan of a book, to contribute to the interesting or elegant distraction of his forlorn and brooding being.

And yet Lothair began to feel uneasy, and his uneasiness increased proportionately as his health improved. He sometimes thought that he should like to make an effort and get about a little in the world; but he was very weak, and without any of the resources to which he had been accustomed throughout life. He had no servants of his own, no carriages, no man of business, no banker; and when at last he tried to bring himself to write to Mr. Putney Giles—a painful task—Monsignore Catesby offered to undertake his whole correspondence for him, and announced that his medical attendants had declared that he must under no circumstances whatever attempt at present to write a letter. Hitherto he had been without money, which was lavishly supplied for his physicians and other wants; and he would have been without clothes if the most fashionable tailor in Rome, a German, had not been in frequent attendance on him under the direction of Monsignore Catesby, who in fact had organised his wardrobe as he did everything else.

Somehow or other Lothair never seemed alone.
When he woke in the morning the Monsignore was
frequently kneeling before an oratory in his room,
and if by any chance Lothair was wanting at Lady
St. Jerome's reception, Father Coleman, who was
now on a visit to the family, would look in and
pass the evening with him, as men who keep a
gaming table find it discreet occasionally to change
the dealer. It is a huge and even stupendous pile—
that Palazzo Agostini, and yet Lothair never tried to
thread his way through its vestibules and galleries,
or attempt a reconnaissance of its endless chambers
without some monsignore or other gliding up quite
apropos, and relieving him from the dullness of solitary existence during the rest of his promenade.

Lothair was relieved by hearing that his former
guardian, Cardinal Grandison, was daily expected at
Rome; and he revolved in his mind whether he
should not speak to his Eminence generally on the
system of his life, which he felt now required some
modification. In the interval, however, no change
did occur. Lothair attended every day the services
of the church, and every evening the receptions of
Lady St. Jerome; and between the discharge of these
two duties he took a drive with a priest—sometimes
with more than one, but always most agreeable men
—generally in the environs of the city, or visited a
convent, or a villa, some beautiful gardens, or a
gallery of works of art.

It was at Lady St. Jerome's that Lothair met his
former guardian. The Cardinal had only arrived in
the morning. His manner to Lothair was affectionate.

He retained Lothair's hand and pressed it with his
pale, thin fingers; his attenuated countenance blazed
for a moment with a divine light.

"I have long wished to see you, sir," said Lothair, "and much wish to talk with you."

"I can hear nothing from you nor of you but
what must be most pleasing to me," said the Cardinal.

"I wish I could believe that," said Lothair.

The Cardinal caressed him; put his arm round
Lothair's neck and said, "There is no time like the
present. Let us walk together in this gallery," and
they withdrew naturally from the immediate scene.

"You know all that has happened, I daresay,"
said Lothair with embarrassment and with a sigh,
"since we parted in England, sir."

"All," said the Cardinal. "It has been a most
striking and merciful dispensation."

"Then I need not dwell upon it," said Lothair,
"and naturally it would be most painful. What I
wish particularly to speak to you about is my position under this roof. What I owe to those who dwell
under it no language can describe, and no efforts
on my part, and they shall be unceasing, can repay.
But I think the time has come when I ought no
longer to trespass on their affectionate devotion,
though, when I allude to the topic, they seem to
misinterpret the motives which influence me, and to
be pained rather than relieved by my suggestions. I
cannot bear being looked upon as ungrateful, when
in fact I am devoted to them. I think, sir, you
might help me in putting all this right."

"If it be necessary," said the Cardinal; "but I apprehend you misconceive them. When I last left Rome you were very ill, but Lady St. Jerome and others have written to me almost daily about you during my absence, so that I am familiar with all that has occurred, and quite cognisant of their feelings. Rest assured that, towards yourself, they are exactly what they ought to be and what you would desire."

"Well I am glad," said Lothair, "that you are acquainted with everything that has happened, for you can put them right if it be necessary; but I sometimes cannot help fancying that they are under some false impression both as to my conduct and my convictions."

"Not in the slightest," said the Cardinal, "trust me, my dear friend, for that. They know everything and appreciate everything; and great as, no doubt, have been your sufferings, feel that everything has been ordained for the best; that the hand of the Almighty has been visible throughout all these strange events; that His Church was never more clearly built upon a rock than at this moment; that this great manifestation will revive, and even restore, the faith of Christendom; and that you yourself must be looked upon as one of the most favoured of men."

"Everybody says that," said Lothair rather peevishly.

"And everybody feels it," said the Cardinal.

"Well, to revert to lesser points," said Lothair, "I do not say I want to return to England, for I

dread returning to England, and do not know
whether I shall ever go back there; and at any rate
I doubt not my health at present is unequal to the
effort; but I should like some change in my mode
of life. I will not say it is too much controlled, for
nothing seems ever done without first consulting me;
but, some how or other, we are always in the same
groove. I wish to see more of the world; I wish to
see Rome, and the people of Rome. I wish to see
and do many things which, if I mention, it would
seem to hurt the feelings of others, and my own are
misconceived, but if mentioned by you all would
probably be different."

"I understand you, my dear young friend, my
child, I will still say," said the Cardinal. "Nothing
can be more reasonable than what you suggest. No
doubt our friends may be a little too anxious about
you, but they are the best people in the world. You
appear to me to be quite well enough now to make
more exertion than hitherto they have thought you
capable of. They see you every day, and cannot
judge so well of you as I who have been absent. I
will charge myself to effect all your wishes. And
we will begin by my taking you out to-morrow and
your driving with me about the city. I will show
you Rome and the Roman people."

` Accordingly, on the morrow, Cardinal Grandison
and his late pupil visited together Rome and the
Romans. And first of all Lothair was presented to
the Cardinal Prefect of the Propaganda, who presides over the ecclesiastical affairs of every country
in which the Roman Church has a mission, and that

includes every land between the Arctic and the
Southern Pole. This glimpse of the organised correspondence with both the Americas, all Asia, all
Africa, all Australia, and many European countries,
carried on by a countless staff of clerks in one of
the most capacious buildings in the world, was calculated to impress the visitor with a due idea of the
extensive authority of the Roman Pontiff. This institution, greater, according to the Cardinal, than
any which existed in ancient Rome, was to pro-
pagate the faith, the purity of which the next establishment they visited was to maintain. According
to Cardinal Grandison there never was a body the
character of which had been so wilfully and so ma-
lignantly misrepresented as that of the Roman Inquisition. Its true object is reformation not punish-
ment, and therefore pardon was sure to follow the
admission of error. True is was there were revolting
stories afloat, for which there was undoubtedly some
foundation, though their exaggeration and malice
were evident, of the ruthless conduct of the Inquisition; but these details were entirely confined to
Spain, and were the consequences not of the principles of the Holy Office, but of the Spanish race,
poisoned by Moorish and Jewish blood, or by long
contact with those inhuman infidels. Had it not
been for the Inquisition organising and directing the
mitigating influences of the Church, Spain would
have been a land of wild beasts; and even in quite
modern times it was the Holy Office at Rome which
always stepped forward to protect the persecuted,
and, by the power of appeal from Madrid to Rome,

saved the lives of those who were unjustly or extra-
vagantly accused.

"The real business however of the Holy Office
now," continued the Cardinal, "is in reality only
doctrinal; and there is something truly sublime,
essentially divine, I would say, in this idea of an
old man, like the Holy Father, himself the object of
ceaseless persecution by all the children of Satan,
never for a moment relaxing his heaven-inspired
efforts to maintain the purity of the faith once delivered to the Saints, and at the same time to pro-
pagate it throughout the whole world, so that there
should be no land on which the sun shines that
should not afford means of salvation to suffering
man.   Yes, the Propaganda and the Inquisition
alone are sufficient to vindicate the sacred claims of
Rome.   Compared with them mere secular and
human institutions, however exalted, sink into insignificance."

These excursions with the Cardinal were not only
repeated, but became almost of daily occurrence.
The Cardinal took Lothair with him in his visits of
business, and introduced him to the eminent characters of the city.   Some of these priests were illustrious scholars, or votaries of science, whose
names were quoted with respect and as authority in
the circles of cosmopolitan philosophy.   Then there
were other institutions at Rome, which the Cardinal
snatched occasions to visit, and which, if not so
awfully venerable as the Propaganda and the Inquisition, nevertheless testified to the advanced civilisation of Rome and the Romans, and the enlightened

administration of the Holy Father. According to Cardinal Grandison, all the great modern improvements in the administration of hospitals and prisons originated in the eternal city; scientific ventilation, popular lavatories, the cellular or silent system, the reformatory. And yet these were nothing compared with the achievements of the Pontifical Government in education. In short, complete popular education only existed at Rome. Its schools were more numerous even than its fountains. Gratuitous instruction originated with the ecclesiastics; and from the night school to the university here might be found the perfect type.

"I really believe," said the Cardinal, "that a more virtuous, a more religious, a more happy and contented people than the Romans never existed. They could all be kept in order with the police of one of your counties. True it is the Holy Father is obliged to garrison the city with twelve thousand men of all arms, but not against the Romans, not against his own subjects. It is the Secret Societies of Atheism who have established their lodges in this city, entirely consisting of foreigners, that render these lamentable precautions necessary. They will not rest until they have extirpated the religious principle from the soul of man, and until they have reduced him to the condition of wild beasts. But they will fail, as they failed the other day, as Sennacherib failed. These men may conquer Zouaves and Cuirassiers, but they cannot fight against Saint Michael and all the Angels. They may do mischief, they may aggravate and prolong the misery of man, but they are doomed to entire and eternal failure."

CHAPTER XIX.

LADY ST. JEROME was much interested in the accounts which the Cardinal and Lothair gave her of their excursions in the city and their visits.

"It is very true," she said, "I never knew such good people; and they ought to be; so favoured by Heaven, and leading a life which, if anything earthly can, must give them, however faint, some foretaste of our joys hereafter. Did your Eminence visit the Pellegrini?" This was the hospital where Miss Arundel had found Lothair.

The Cardinal looked grave. "No," he replied. "My object was to secure for our young friend some interesting but not agitating distraction from certain ideas which, however admirable and transcendently important, are nevertheless too high and profound to permit their constant contemplation with impunity to our infirm natures. Besides," he added, in a lower, but still distinct tone, "I was myself unwilling to visit in a mere casual manner the scene of what I must consider the greatest event to this century."

"But you have been there?" enquired Lady St. Jerome.

His Eminence crossed himself.

In the course of the evening Monsignore Catesby

told Lothair that a grand service was about to be
celebrated at the church of St. George: thanks were
to be offered to the Blessed Virgin by Miss Arundel
for the miraculous mercy vouchsafed to her in saving the life of a countryman, Lothair. "All her
friends will make a point of being there," added the
Monsignore, "even the Protestants and some Russians. Miss Arundel was very unwilling at first to
fulfil this office, but the Holy Father has commanded
it. I know that nothing will induce her to ask you
to attend; and yet, if I were you, I would turn it
over in your mind. I know she said that she would
sooner that you were present than all her English
friends together. However, you can think about it.
One likes to do what is proper."

One does; and yet it is difficult. Sometimes in
doing what we think proper, we get into irremediable
scrapes; and often, what we hold to be proper,
society in its caprice resolves to be highly improper.

Lady St. Jerome had wished Lothair to see
Tivoli, and they were all consulting together when
they might go there. Lord St. Jerome who, besides
his hunters, had his drag at Rome, wanted to drive
them to the place. Lothair sate opposite Miss
Arundel, gazing on her beauty. It was like being
at Vauxe again. And yet a great deal had happened since they were at Vauxe; and what? So far
as they two were concerned, nothing but what
should create or confirm relations of confidence and
affection. Whatever may have been the influence of
others on his existence, hers at least had been one
of infinite benignity. She had saved his life, she

had cherished it. She had raised him from the lowest depth of physical and moral prostration to health and comparative serenity. If at Vauxe he had beheld her with admiration, had listened with fascinated interest to the fervid expression of her saintly thoughts, and the large purposes of her heroic mind, all these feelings were naturally heightened now when he had witnessed her lofty and consecrated spirit in action, and when that action in his own case had only been exercised for his ineffable advantage.

"Your uncle cannot go to-morrow," continued Lady St. Jerome, "and on Thursday I am engaged."

"And on Friday——" said Miss Arundel, hesitating.

"We are all engaged," said Lady St. Jerome.

"I should hardly wish to go out before Friday anywhere," said Miss Arundel, speaking to her aunt, and in a lower tone.

Friday was the day on which the thanksgiving service was to be celebrated in the Jesuit church of St. George of Cappadocia. Lothair knew this well enough and was embarrassed: a thanksgiving for the mercy vouchsafed to Miss Arundel in saving the life of a fellow-countryman, and that fellow-countryman not present! All her Protestant friends would be there, and some Russians. And he not there! It seemed, on his part, the most ungracious and intolerable conduct. And he knew that she would prefer his presence to that of all her acquaintances

together. It was more than ungracious on his part;
it was ungrateful, almost inhuman.

Lothair sate silent, and stupid, and stiff, and dissatisfied with himself.   Once or twice he tried to
speak, but his tongue would not move, or his throat
was not clear.   And if he had spoken, he would
only have made some trifling and awkward remark.
In his mind's eye he saw, gliding about him, the
veiled figure of his sick room, and he recalled with
clearness the unceasing and angelic tenderness of
which at the time he seemed hardly conscious.

Miss Arundel had risen and had proceeded some
way down the room to a cabinet where she was accustomed to place her work.   Suddenly Lothair rose
and followed her.   "Miss Arundel!" he said, and
she looked round, hardly stopping when he had
reached her.   "Miss Arundel, I hope you will permit
me to be present at the celebration on Friday?"

She turned round quickly, extending, even
eagerly, her hand with mantling cheek.   Her eyes
glittered with celestial fire.   The words hurried from
her palpitating lips: "And support me," she said,
"for I need support."

In the evening reception, Monsignore Catesby
approached Father Coleman.   "It is done," he said,
with a look of saintly triumph.   "It is done at last.
He will not only be present, but he will support her.
There are yet eight and forty hours to elapse.   Can
anything happen to defeat us?   It would seem not;
yet when so much is at stake, one is fearful.   He
must never be out of our sight; not a human being
must approach him."

"I think we can manage that," said Father Coleman.

CHAPTER XX.

THE Jesuit church of St. George of Cappadocia was situate in one of the finest piazzas of Rome. It was surrounded with arcades, and in its centre the most beautiful fountain of the city spouted forth its streams to an amazing height, and in forms of graceful fancy. On Friday morning the arcades were festooned with tapestry and hangings of crimson velvet and gold. Every part was crowded, and all the rank and fashion and power of Rome seemed to be there assembling. There had been once some intention on the part of the Holy Father to be present, but a slight indisposition had rendered that not desirable. His Holiness, however, had ordered a company of his halberdiers to attend, and the ground was kept by those wonderful guards in the dress of the middle ages—halberds and ruffs, and white plumes, and party-coloured coats, a match for our beefeaters. Carriages with scarlet umbrellas on the box, and each with three serving men behind, denoted the presence of the cardinals in force. They were usually brilliant equipages, being sufficiently new, or sufficiently new purchases, Garibaldi and the late commanding officer of Lothair having burnt most of the ancient coaches in the time of the Roman Republic twenty years before. From each car-

9*

riage an eminence descended with his scarlet cap
and his purple train borne by two attendants. The
Princess Tarpeia-Cinque Cento was there, and most
of the Roman princes and princesses and dukes and
duchesses. It seemed that the whole court of Rome
was there—monsignori and prelates without end.
Some of their dresses, and those of the generals of
the orders, appropriately varied the general effect,
for the ladies were all in black, their heads covered
only with black veils.

Monsignore Catesby had arranged with Lothair
that they should enter the church by their usual
private way, and Lothair therefore was not in any
degree prepared for the sight which awaited him on
his entrance into it. The church was crowded; not
a chair nor a tribune vacant. There was a sup-
pressed gossip going on as in a public place before
a performance begins, much fluttering of fans, some
snuff taken, and many sugar plums.

"Where shall we find a place?" said Lothair.

"They expect us in the sacristy," said the Monsignore.

The sacristy of the Jesuit church of St. George
of Cappadocia might have served for the ball-room
of a palace. It was lofty, and proportionately spacious, with a grooved ceiling painted with all the court
of heaven. Above the broad and richly gilt cornice
floated a company of Seraphim that might have
figured as the Cupids of Albano. The apartment
was crowded, for there and in some adjoining
chambers were assembled the cardinals and prelates,
and all the distinguished or official characters, who,

in a few minutes, were about to form a procession
of almost unequal splendour and sanctity, and which
was to parade the whole body of the church.

Lothair felt nervous; an indefinable depression
came over him, as on the morning of a contest
when a candidate enters his crowded committee-
room. Considerable personages bowing, approached
to address him—the Cardinal Prefect of the Propaganda, the Cardinal Assessor of the Holy Office, the
Cardinal Pro-Datario, and the Cardinal Vicar of
Rome. Monsignori the Secretary of Briefs to Princes
and the Master of the Apostolic Palace were presented to him.   Had this been a conclave, and Lothair the future Pope, it would have been impossible
to have treated him with more consideration than he
experienced.   They assured him that they looked
upon this day as one of the most interesting in their
lives, and the importance of which to the Church
could not be overrated.   All this somewhat encouraged him, and he was more himself when a certain general stir, and the entrance of individuals
from adjoining apartments, intimated that the proceedings were about to commence.   It seemed difficult to marshal so considerable and so stately an assemblage, but those who had the management of
affairs were experienced in such matters.   The aco-
lytes and the thurifers fell into their places; there
seemed no end of banners and large golden crosses;
great was the company of the prelates—a long purple
line, some only in cassocks, some in robes, and
mitred; then came a new banner of the Blessed
Virgin, which excited intense interest, and every eye

was strained to catch the pictured scene. After this
banner, amid frequent incense, walked two of the
most beautiful children in Rome, dressed as angels
with golden wings; the boy bearing a rose of Jericho,
the girl a lily. After these, as was understood,
dressed in black and veiled, walked six ladies, who
were said to be daughters of the noblest houses of
England, and then a single form with a veil touching the ground.

"Here we must go," said Monsignore Catesby to
Lothair, and he gently but irresistibly pushed him
into his place. "You know you promised to support
her. You had better take this," he said, thrusting
a lighted taper into his hand; "it is usual, and one
should never be singular."

So they walked on, followed by the Roman princes, bearing a splendid baldachin. And then came
the pomp of the cardinals, each with his train-bearers,
exhibiting with the skill of artists the splendour of
their violet robes.

As the head of the procession emerged from the
sacristy into the church, three organs and a choir,
to which all the Roman churches had lent their
choicest voices, burst into the Te Deum. Round
the church and to all the chapels, and then up the
noble nave, the majestic procession moved, and then
the gates of the holy place opening, the cardinals
entered and seated themselves, their train-bearers
crouching at their knees, the prelates grouped themselves, and the banners and crosses were ranged in
the distance, except the new banner of the Virgin,
which seemed to hang over the altar. The Holy

One seemed to be in what was recently a field of battle, and was addressing a beautiful maiden in the dress of a Sister of Mercy.

"This is your place," said Monsignore Catesby, and he pushed Lothair into a prominent position.

The service was long, but sustained by exquisite music, celestial perfumes, and the graceful movements of priests in resplendent dresses continually changing, it could not be said to be wearisome. When all was over, Monsignore Catesby said to Lothair, "I think we had better return by the public way; it seems expected."

It was not easy to leave the church. Lothair was detained, and received the congratulations of the Princess Tarpeia-Cinque Cento and many others. The crowd, much excited by the carriages of the cardinals, had not diminished when they came forth, and they were obliged to linger some little time upon the steps, the Monsignore making difficulties when Lothair more than once proposed to advance.

"I think we may go now," said Catesby, and they descended into the piazza. Immediately many persons in their immediate neighbourhood fell upon their knees, many asked a blessing from Lothair, and some rushed forward to kiss the hem of his garment.

CHAPTER XXI.

THE Princess Tarpeia-Cinque Cento gave an
entertainment in the evening in honour of "the great
event." Italian palaces are so vast, are so ill-adapted
to the moderate establishments of modern times, that
their grand style in general only impresses those who
visit them with a feeling of disappointment and even
mortification. The meagre retinue are almost invisible as they creep about the corridors and galleries,
and linger in the sequence of lofty chambers. These
should be filled with crowds of serving men and
groups of splendid retainers. They were built for
the days when a great man was obliged to have a
great following; and when the safety of his person,
as well as the success of his career, depended on
the number and the lustre of his train.

The palace of the Princess Tarpeia was the most
celebrated in Rome, one of the most ancient, and
certainly the most beautiful. She dwelt in it in a
manner not unworthy of her consular blood and her
modern income. To-night her guests were received
by a long line of foot servants in showy liveries, and
bearing the badge of her house, while in every convenient spot pages and gentlemen ushers in courtly
dress guided the guests to their place of destination.
The palace blazed with light, and showed to advantage the thousand pictures which, it is said, were

there enshrined, and the long galleries full of the pale statues of Grecian gods and goddesses and the busts of the former rulers of Rome and the Romans. The atmosphere was fragrant with rare odours, and music was heard amid the fall of fountains in the dim but fancifully illumined gardens.

The Princess herself wore all those famous jewels which had been spared by all the Goths from the days of Brennus to those of Garibaldi, and on her bosom reposed the celebrated transparent cameo of Augustus, which Cæsar himself is said to have presented to Livia, and which Benvenuto Cellini had set in a framework of Cupids and rubies. If the weight of her magnificence were sometimes distressing, she had the consolation of being supported by the arm of Lothair.

Two young Roman princes, members of the Guarda Nobile, discussed the situation.

"The English here say," said one, "that he is their richest man."

"And very noble, too," said the other.

"Certainly, truly noble—a kind of cousin of the Queen."

"This great event must have an effect upon all their nobility. I cannot doubt they will all return to the Holy Father."

"They would if they were not afraid of having to restore their church lands. But they would be much more happy if Rome were again the capital of the world."

"No shadow of doubt. I wonder if this young prince will hunt in the Campagna?"

"All Englishmen hunt."

"I make no doubt he rides well, and has famous horses, and will sometimes lend us one. I am glad his soul is saved."

"Yes; it is well, when the Blessed Virgin interferes, it should be in favour of princes. When princes become good Christians it is an example. It does good. And this man will give an impulse to our opera, which wants it, and, as you say, he will have many horses."

In the course of the evening Miss Arundel, with a beaming face but of deep expression, said to Lothair, "I could tell you some good news had I not promised the Cardinal that he should communicate it to you himself. He will see you to-morrow. Although it does not affect me personally, it will be to me the happiest event that ever occurred, except, of course, one."

"What can she mean?" thought Lothair. But at that moment Cardinal Berwick approached him, and Miss Arundel glided away.

Father Coleman attended Lothair home to the Agostini Palace, and when they parted said with much emphasis, "I must congratulate you once more on the great event."

On the following morning, Lothair found on his table a number of the Roman journal published that day. It was customary to place it there, but in general he only glanced at it, and scarcely that. On the present occasion his own name caught immediately his eye. It figured in a long account of the celebration of the preceding day. It was with a continually changing countenance, now scarlet, now pallid as death; with a palpitating heart, a trembling hand, a cold perspiration, and at length a disordered vision, that Lothair read the whole of an article, of which we now give a summary:

"Rome was congratulated on the service of yesterday which celebrated the greatest event of this century. And it came to pass in this wise. It seems that a young English noble, of the highest rank, family, and fortune (and here the name and titles of Lothair were accurately given), like many of the scions of the illustrious and influential families of Britain, was impelled by an irresistible motive to enlist as a volunteer in the service of the Pope, when the Holy Father was recently attacked by the Secret Societies of Atheism. This gallant and gifted youth, after prodigies of valour and devotion, had fallen at Mentana in the sacred cause, and was given up for lost. The day after the battle, when the ambulances laden with the wounded were hourly arriving at Rome from the field, an English lady, daughter of an illustrious house, celebrated throughout centuries for its devotion to the Holy See, and who during the present awful trial had never ceased in her efforts to support the cause of Christianity, was employed, as was her wont, in offices of charity, and was tending with her companion sisters her wounded countrymen at the hospital La Consolazione, in the new ward which has been recently added to that establishment by the Holy Father.

"While she was leaning over one of the beds, she felt a gentle and peculiar pressure on her

shoulder, and, looking round, beheld a most beautiful woman, with a countenance of singular sweetness
and yet majesty.   And the visitor said, 'You are
attending to those English who believe in the Virgin
Mary.   Now at the Hospital Santissima Trinitá di
Pellegrini there is in an ambulance a young Englishman apparently dead, but who will not die if you
go to him immediately and say you came in the
name of the Virgin.'

"The influence of the stranger was so irresistible
that the young English lady, attended by a nurse
and one of the porters of La Consolazione, repaired
instantly to the Di Pellegrini, and there they found
in the courtyard, as they had been told, an
ambulance, in form and colour and equipment unlike
any ambulance used by the papal troops, and in the
ambulance the senseless body of a youth, who was
recognised by the English lady as her young and
gallant countryman.   She claimed him in the name
of the Blessed Virgin, and, after due remedies, was
permitted to take him at once to his noble relatives,
who lived in the Palazzo Agostini.

"After a short time much conversation began to
circulate about this incident.   The family wished to
testify their gratitude to the individual whose information had led to the recovery of the body, and
subsequently of the life of their relation; but all that
they could at first learn at La Consolazione was,
that the porter believed the woman was Maria Serafina di Angelis, the handsome wife of a tailor in the
Strada di Ripetta.   But it was soon shown that this
could not be true, for it was proved that, on the

day in question, Maria Serafina di Angelis was on a
visit to a friend at La Riccia; and, in the second
place, that she did not bear the slightest resemblance to the stranger who had given the news.
Moreover, the porter of the gate being required to
state why he had admitted any stranger without the
accustomed order, denied that he had so done; that
he was in his lodge and the gates were locked, and
the stranger had passed through without his knowledge.

"Two priests were descending the stairs when
the stranger came upon them, and they were so
struck by the peculiarity of her carriage, that they
turned round and looked at her, and clearly observed at the back of her head a sort of halo. She
was out of their sight when they made this observation, but in consequence of it they made enquiries
of the porter of the gate, and remained in the courtyard till she returned.

"This she did a few minutes before the English
lady and her attendants came down, as they had
been detained by the preparation of some bandages
and other remedies, without which they never moved.
The porter of the gate having his attention called to
the circumstance by the priests, was most careful in
his observations as to the halo, and described it as
most distinct. The priests then followed the stranger,
who proceeded down a long and solitary street,
made up in a great degree of garden and convent
walls, and without a turning. They observed her
stop and speak to two children, and then, though
there was no house to enter and no street to turn
into, she vanished.

"When they had reached the children they found each of them holding in its hand a beautiful flower. It seems the lady had given the boy a rose of Jericho, and to his sister a white and golden lily. Enquiring whether she had spoken to them, they answered that she had said, 'Let these flowers be kept in remembrance of me; they will never fade.' And truly, though months had elapsed, these flowers had never faded, and, after the procession of yesterday, they were placed under crystal in the chapel of the Blessed Virgin in the Jesuit church of St. George of Cappadocia, and may be seen every day, and will be seen for ever in primeval freshness.

"This is the truthful account of what really occurred with respect to this memorable event, and as it was ascertained by a Consulta of the Holy Office, presided over by the Cardinal Prefect himself. The Holy Office is most severe in its inquisition of the truth, and though it well knows that the Divine presence never leaves His Church, it is most scrupulous in its investigations whenever any miraculous interposition is alleged. It was entirely by its exertions that the somewhat inconsistent and unsatisfactory evidence of the porter of the gate, in the first instance, was explained, cleared, and established; the whole chain of evidence worked out; all idle gossip and mere rumours rejected; and the evidence obtained of above twenty witnesses of all ranks of life, some of them members of the learned profession, and others military officers of undoubted honour and veracity, who witnessed the first appearance of the stranger at the Pellegrini, and the undoubted fact of the halo playing round her temples.

"The Consulta of the Holy Office could only draw one inference, sanctioned by the Holy Father himself, as to the character of the personage who thus deigned to appear and interpose; and no wonder that in the great function of yesterday, the eyes of all Rome were fixed upon Lothair as the most favoured of living men."

He himself now felt as one sinking into an unfathomable abyss. The despair came over him that involves a man engaged in a hopeless contest with a remorseless power. All his life during the last year passed rushingly across his mind. He recalled the wiles that had been employed to induce him to attend a function in a Jesuits' chapel in an obscure nook of London; the same agencies had been employed there; then, as now, the influence of Clare Arundel had been introduced to sway him when all others had failed. Belmont had saved him then. There was no Belmont now. The last words of Theodora murmured in his ear like the awful voice of a distant sea. They were the diapason of all the thought and feeling of that profound and passionate spirit.

That seemed only a petty plot in London, and he had since sometimes smiled when he remembered how it had been baffled. Shallow apprehension! The petty plot was only part of a great and unceasing and triumphant conspiracy, and the obscure and inferior agencies which he had been rash enough to deride had consummated their commanded purpose in the eyes of all Europe, and with the aid of the great powers of the world.

He felt all the indignation natural to a sincere and high-spirited man, who finds that he has been befooled by those whom he has trusted; but summoning all his powers to extricate himself from his desolate dilemma, he found himself without resource. What public declaration on his part could alter the undeniable fact, now circulating throughout the world, that in the supernatural scene of yesterday he was the willing and the principal actor? Unquestionably he had been very imprudent, not only in that instance but in his habitual visits to the church; he felt all that now. But he was torn and shattered, infinitely distressed both in body and in mind; weak and miserable; and he thought he was leaning on angelic hearts, when he found himself in the embrace of spirits of another sphere.

In what a position of unexampled pain did he not now find himself! To feel it your duty to quit the faith in which you have been bred must involve an awful pang; but to be a renegade without the consolation of conscience, against your sense, against your will, alike for no celestial hope and no earthly object, this was agony mixed with self-contempt.

He remembered what Lady Corisande had once said to him about those who quitted their native church for the Roman communion. What would she say now? He marked in imagination the cloud of sorrow on her imperial brow and the scorn of her curled lip.

Whatever happened he could never return to England—at least for many years, when all the things and persons he cared for would have disappeared, or changed, which is worse; and then what would be the use of returning? He would go to America, or Australia, or the Indian Ocean, or the interior of Africa; but even in all these places, according to the correspondence of the Propaganda, he would find Roman priests and active priests. He felt himself a lost man; not free from faults in this matter, but punished beyond his errors. But this is the fate of men who think they can struggle successfully with a supernatural power.

A servant opened a door and said in a loud voice, that, with his permission, his Eminence, the English Cardinal, would wait on him.

CHAPTER XXII.

It is proverbial to what drowning men will cling. Lothair, in his utter hopelessness, made a distinction between the Cardinal and the conspirators. The Cardinal had been absent from Rome during the greater portion of the residence of Lothair in that city. The Cardinal was his father's friend, an English gentleman, with an English education, once an Anglican, a man of the world, a man of honour, a good, kind-hearted man. Lothair explained the apparent and occasional co-operation of his Eminence with the others, by their making use of him without

a due consciousness of their purpose on his part.
Lothair remembered how delicately his former
guardian had always treated the subject of religion
in their conversations. The announcement of his visit
instead of aggravating the distresses of Lothair,
seemed, as all these considerations rapidly occured
to him, almost to impart a ray of hope.

"I see," said the Cardinal, as he entered serene
and graceful as usual, and glancing at the table,
"that you have been reading the account of our
great act of yesterday."

"Yes; and I have been reading it," said Lothair
reddening, "with indignation; with alarm; I should
add, with disgust."

"How is this?" said the Cardinal feeling or af-
fecting surprise.

"It is a tissue of falsehood and imposture," continued Lothair; "and I will take care that my opinion
is known of it."

"Do nothing rashly," said the Cardinal. "This
is an official journal, and I have reason to believe
that nothing appears in it which is not drawn up,
or well considered, by truly pious men."

"You yourself, sir, must know," continued Lothair,
"that the whole of this statement is founded on
falsehood."

"Indeed I should be sorry to believe," said the
Cardinal, "that there was a particle of misstatement,
or even exaggeration, either in the base or the super-
structure of the narrative."

"Good God!" exclaimed Lothair. "Why take
the very first allegation, that I fell at Mentana fight-

ing in the ranks of the Holy Father. Every one
knows that I fell fighting against him, and that I
was almost slain by one of his chassepots. It is
notorious; and though, as a matter of taste, I have
not obtruded the fact in the society in which I have
been recently living, I have never attempted to conceal it, and have not the slightest doubt that it must
be as familiar to every member of that society as to
your Eminence."

"I know there are two narratives of your relations
with the battle of Mentana," observed the Cardinal
quietly. "The one accepted as authentic is that
which appears in this journal; the other account,
which can only be traced to yourself, bears no
doubt a somewhat different character; but considering that it is in the highest degree improbable, and
that there is not a tittle of confirmatory or collateral
evidence to extenuate its absolute unlikelihood, I
hardly think you are justified in using, with reference
to the statement in this article, the harsh expression
which I am persuaded, on reflection, you will feel
you have hastily used."

"I think," said Lothair with a kindling eye and
a burning cheek, "that I am the best judge of what
I did at Mentana."

"Well, well," said the Cardinal with dulcet calm-
ness, "you naturally think so; but you must remember you have been very ill, my dear young
friend, and labouring under much excitement. If I
were you, and I speak as your friend, I hope your
best one, I would not dwell too much on this fancy
of yours about the battle of Mentana. I would

myself always deal tenderly with a fixed idea: harsh attempts to terminate hallucination are seldom successful. Nevertheless, in the case of a public event, a matter of fact, if a man finds that he is of one opinion and all orders of society of another, he should not be encouraged to dwell on a perverted view; he should be gradually weaned from it."

"You amaze me!" said Lothair.

"Not at all," said the Cardinal. "I am sure you will benefit by my advice. And you must already perceive that, assuming the interpretation which the world without exception places on your conduct in the field to be the just one, there really is not a single circumstance in the whole of this interesting and important statement, the accuracy of which you yourself would for a moment dispute."

"What is there said about me at Mentana makes me doubt of all the rest," said Lothair.

"Well, we will not dwell on Mentana," said the Cardinal with a sweet smile; "I have treated of that point. Your case is by no means an uncommon one. It will wear off with returning health. King George IV. believed that he was at the battle of Waterloo, and indeed commanded there; and his friends were at one time a little alarmed; but Knighton, who was a sensible man, said, 'His Majesty has only to leave off Curaçoa, and rest assured he will gain no more victories.' The rest of this statement, which is to-day officially communicated to the whole world, and which in its results will probably be not less important even than the celebration of the Centenary of St. Peter, is established

by evidence so incontestable—by witnesses so numerous, so various—in all the circumstances and
accidents of testimony so satisfactory—I may say so
irresistible, that controversy on this head would be
a mere impertinence and waste of time."

"I am not convinced," said Lothair.

"Hush!" said the Cardinal, "the freaks of your
own mind about personal incidents, however lamentable, may be viewed with indulgence—at least for
a time.   But you cannot be permitted to doubt of
the rest.   You must be convinced, and on reflection
you will be convinced.   Remember, sir, where you
are.   You are in the centre of Christendom, where
truth, and where alone truth resides.   Divine authority has perused this paper and approved it.   It is
published for the joy and satisfaction of two hundred
millions of Christians, and for the salvation of all
those who unhappily for themselves are not yet con-
verted to the faith.   It records the most memorable
event of this century.   Our Blessed Lady has personally appeared to her votaries before during that
period, but never at Rome.   Wisely and well she
has worked in villages and among the illiterate as
at the beginning did her Divine Son.   But the time
is now ripe for terminating the infidelity of the
world.   In the eternal city, amid all its matchless
learning and profound theology, in the sight of
thousands, this great act has been accomplished, in
a manner which can admit of no doubt, and which
can lead to no controversy.   Some of the most
notorious atheists of Rome have already solicited to
be admitted to the offices of the Church; the Secret

Societies have received their death-blow; I look to
the alienation of England as virtually over. I am
panting to see you return to the home of your fathers
and reconquer it for the Church in the name of the
Lord God of Sabaoth.   Never was a man in a greater
position since Godfrey or Ignatius.   The eyes of all
Christendom are upon you as the most favoured of
men, and you stand there like Saint Thomas."

"Perhaps he was as bewildered as I am," said
Lothair.

"Well, his bewilderment ended in his becoming
an apostle, as yours will.   I am glad we have had
this conversation and that we agree; I knew we
should.   But now I wish to speak to you on business,
and very grave.   The world assumes that being the
favoured of Heaven you are naturally and necessarily
a member of the Church.   I, your late guardian,
know that is not the case, and sometimes I blame
myself that it is not so.   But I have ever scrupulously refrained from attempting to control your convictions; and the result has justified me.   Heaven
has directed your life, and I have now to impart to
you the most gratifying intelligence that can be communicated by man, and that the Holy Father will
to-morrow himself receive you into the bosom of
that Church of which he is the divine head.   Christendom will then hail you as its champion and regen-
erator, and thus will be realised the divine dream
with which you were inspired in our morning walk
in the park at Vauxe."

CHAPTER XXIII.

IT was the darkest hour in Lothair's life. He had become acquainted with sorrow; he had experienced calamities physical and moral. The death of Theodora had shaken him to the centre. It was that first great grief which makes a man acquainted with his deepest feelings, which detracts something from the buoyancy of the youngest life, and dims, to a certain degree, the lustre of existence. But even that bereavement was mitigated by distractions alike inevitable and ennobling. The sternest and highest of all obligations, military duty, claimed him with an unfaltering grasp, and the clarion sounded almost as he closed her eyes. Then he went forth to struggle for a cause which at least she believed to be just and sublime; and if his own convictions on that head might be less assured or precise, still there was doubtless much that was inspiring in the contest, and much dependent on the success of himself and his comrades that tended to the elevation of man.

But, now, there was not a single circumstance to sustain his involved and sinking life. A renegade —a renegade without conviction, without necessity, in absolute violation of the pledge he had given to the person he most honoured and most loved, as he received her parting spirit! And why was all this?

and how was all this? What system of sorcery had
encompassed his existence?   For he was spell-bound
—as much as any knight in fairy tale whom malig-
nant influences had robbed of his valour and will
and virtue.   No sane person could credit, even
comprehend, his position.   Had he the opportunity
of stating it in a court of justice to-morrow, he
could only enter into a narrative which would decide
his lot as an insane being.   The magical rites had
been so gradual, so subtle, so multifarious, all in
appearance independent of each other, though in
reality scientifically combined, that while the conspirators had probably effected his ruin both in body
and in soul, the only charges he could make against
them would be acts of exquisite charity, tenderness,
self-sacrifice, personal devotion, refined piety, and
religious sentiment of the most exalted character.

What was to be done?   And could anything be
done?   Could he escape?   Where from and where
to?   He was certain, and had been for some time,
from many circumstances, that he was watched.
Could he hope that the vigilance which observed all
his movements would scruple to prevent any which
might be inconvenient?   He felt assured that, to
quit that palace alone, was not in his power.   And
were it, whither could he go?   To whom was he to
appeal?   And about what was he to appeal?   Should .
he appeal to the Holy Father?   There would be an
opportunity for that to-morrow.   To the College of
Cardinals, who had solemnised yesterday with gracious unction his spiritual triumph?   To those con-
genial spirits, the mild Assessor of the Inquisition,

or the President of the Propaganda, who was busied
at that moment in circulating throughout both the
Americas, all Asia, all Africa, all Australia, and
parts of Europe, for the edification of distant millions, the particulars of the miraculous scene in which
he was the principal actor?   Should he throw himself on the protection of the ambiguous minister of
the British Crown, and invoke his aid against a conspiracy touching the rights, reason, and freedom of
one of Her Majesty's subjects?   He would probably
find that functionary inditing a private letter to the
English Secretary of State, giving the minister a
graphic account of the rare doings of yesterday, and
assuring the minister, from his own personal and
ocular experience, that a member of one of the
highest orders of the British peerage carried in the
procession a lighted taper after two angels with
amaranthine flowers and golden wings.

Lothair remained in his apartments; no one approached him.   It was the only day that the Monsignore had not waited on him.   Father Coleman
was equally reserved.   Strange to say, not one of
those agreeable and polite gentlemen, fathers of the
oratory, who talked about gems, torsos, and excava-
tions, and who always more or less attended his
levée, troubled him this morning. With that exquisite
tact which pervades the hierarchical circles of Rome,
everyone felt that Lothair, on the eve of that event
of his life which Providence had so long and so
mysteriously prepared, would wish to be undisturbed.

Restless, disquieted, revolving all the incidents
of his last year, trying, by terrible analysis, to ascer-

tain how he ever could have got into such a false
position, and how he could yet possiby extricate
himself from it, not shrinking in many things from
self-blame, and yet not recognising on his part such
a degree of deviation from the standard of right
feeling, or even of common sense, as would authorise
such an overthrow as that awaiting him—high rank
and boundless wealth, a station of duty and of honour,
some gifts of nature, and golden youth, and a disposition that at least aspired, in the employment of
these accidents of life and fortune, at something
better than selfish gratification, all smashed—the day
drew on.

Drew on the day, and every hour it seemed his
spirit was more lone and dark. For the first time
the thought of death occurred to him as a relief
from the perplexities of existence. How much better
had he died at Mentana! To this pass had arrived
the cordial and brilliant Lord of Muriel, who enjoyed
and adorned life, and wished others to adorn and
to enjoy it; the individual whom, probably, were the
majority of the English people polled, they would
have fixed upon as filling the most enviable of all
positions, and holding out a hope that he was not
unworthy of it. Born with every advantage that
could command the sympathies of his fellow-men,
with a quick intelligence and a noble disposition,
here he was at one-and-twenty ready to welcome
death, perhaps even to devise it, as the only rescue
from a doom of confusion, degradation, and remorse.

He had thrown himself on a sofa, and had buried
his face in his hands to assist the abstraction which

he demanded. There was not an incident of his life that escaped the painful inquisition of his memory. He passed his childhood once more in that stern Scotch home, that, after all, had been so kind, and, as it would seem, so wise. The last words of counsel and of warning from his uncle, expressed at Muriel, came back to him. And yet there seemed a destiny throughout these transactions which was irresistible! The last words of Theodora, her look, even more solemn than her tone, might have been breathed over a tripod, for they were a prophecy, not a warning.

How long he had been absorbed in this passionate reverie he knew not, but when he looked up again it was night, and the moon had touched his window. He rose and walked up and down the room, and then went into the corridor. All was silent; not an attendant was visible; the sky was clear and starry, and the moonlight fell on the tall, still cypresses in the vast quadrangle.

Lothair leant over the balustrade and gazed upon the moonlit fountains. The change of scene, silent and yet not voiceless, and the softening spell of the tranquillising hour were a relief to him. And after a time he wandered about the corridors, and after a time he descended into the court. The tall Swiss, in his grand uniform, was closing the gates which had just released a visitor. Lothair motioned that he too wished to go forth, and the Swiss obeyed him. The threshold was passed, and Lothair found himself for the first time alone in Rome.

Utterly reckless he cared not where he went or

what might happen. The streets were quite deserted, and he wandered about with a strange curiosity, gratified as he sometimes encountered famous objects he had read of, and yet the true character of which no reading ever realises.

The moonlight becomes the proud palaces of Rome, their corniced and balconied fronts rich with deep shadows in the blaze. Sometimes he encountered an imperial column; sometimes he came to an arcadian square flooded with light and resonant with the fall of statued fountains. Emerging from a long straggling street of convents and gardens, he found himself in an open space full of antique ruins, and among them the form of a colossal amphitheatre that he at once recognised.

It rose with its three tiers of arches and the huge wall that crowns them, black and complete in the air; and not until Lothair had entered it could he perceive the portion of the outer wall that was in ruins, and now bathed with the silver light. Lothair was alone. In that huge creation, once echoing with the shouts, and even the agonies, of thousands, Lothair was alone.

He sate him down on a block of stone in that sublime and desolate arena, and asked himself the secret spell of this Rome that had already so agitated his young life, and probably was about critically to affect it. Theodora lived for Rome and died for Rome. And the Cardinal, born and bred an English gentleman, with many hopes and honours, had renounced his religion, and, it might be said, his country, for Rome. And for Rome, to-morrow,

Catesby would die without a pang, and sacrifice himself for Rome, as his race for three hundred years had given, for the same cause, honour and broad estates and unhesitating lives. And these very people were influenced by different motives, and thought they were devoting themselves to opposite ends. But still it was Rome—Republican or Cæsarian, papal or pagan, it still was Rome.

Was it a breeze in a breezeless night that was sighing amid these ruins? A pine tree moved its head on a broken arch, and there was a stir among the plants that hung on the ancient walls. It was a breeze in a breezeless night that was sighing amid the ruins.

There was a tall crag of ancient building contiguous to the block on which Lothair was seated, and which on his arrival he had noted, although, long lost in reverie, he had not recently turned his glance in that direction. He was roused from that reverie by the indefinite sense of some change having occurred which often disturbs and terminates one's brooding thoughts. And looking round, he felt, he saw, he was no longer alone. The moonbeams fell upon a figure that was observing him from the crag of ruin that was near, and as the light clustered and gathered round the form, it became every moment more definite and distinct.

Lothair would have sprung forward, but he could only extend his arms: he would have spoken, but his tongue was paralysed.

"Lothair," said a deep, sweet voice that never could be forgotten.

"I am here," he at last replied.

"Remember;" and she threw upon him that glance, at once serene and solemn, that had been her last, and was impressed indelibly upon his heart of hearts.

Now, he could spring forward and throw himself at her feet, but alas! as he reached her, the figure melted into the moonlight, and she was gone—that divine Theodora, who, let us hope, returned at least to those Elysian fields she so well deserved.

CHAPTER XXIV.

"THEY have overdone it, Gertrude, with Lothair," said Lord St. Jerome to his wife. "I spoke to Monsignore Catesby about it some time ago, but he would not listen to me; I had more confidence in the Cardinal and am disappointed; but a priest is ever too hot. His nervous system has been tried too much."

Lady St. Jerome still hoped the best, and believed in it. She was prepared to accept the way Lothair was found senseless in the Coliseum as a continuance of miraculous Interpositions. He might have remained there for a day or days and never have been recognised when discovered. How marvellously providential that Father Coleman should have been in the vicinity and tempted to visit the great ruin that very night!

Lord St. Jerome was devout, and easy in his temper. Priests and women seemed to have no difficulty in managing him. But he was an English gentleman, and there was at the bottom of his character a fund of courage, firmness, and common sense, that sometimes startled and sometimes perplexed those who assumed that he could be easily controlled. He was not satisfied with the condition of Lothair "a peer of England and my connection;" and he had not unlimited confidence in those who had been hitherto consulted as to his state. There was a celebrated English physician at that time visiting Rome, and Lord St. Jerome, notwithstanding the multiform resistance of Monsignore Catesby, insisted he should be called in to Lothair.

The English physician was one of those men who abhor priests, and do not particularly admire ladies. The latter, in revenge, denounced his manners as brutal, though they always sent for him, and were always trying, though vainly, to pique him into sympathy. He rarely spoke, but he listened to every-one with entire patience. He sometimes asked a question, but he never made a remark.

Lord St. Jerome had seen the physician alone before he visited the Palazzo Agostini, and had talked to him freely about Lothair. The physician saw at once that Lord St. Jerome was truthful, and that though his intelligence might be limited, it was pure and direct. Appreciating Lord St. Jerome, that nobleman found the redoubtable doctor not un-genial, and assured his wife that she would meet on the morrow by no means so savage a being as she anticipated. She received him accordingly, and in the presence of Monsignore Catesby. Never had

she exercised her distinguished powers of social
rhetoric with more art and fervour, and never apparently had they proved less productive of the intended consequences.   The physician said not a
word, and merely bowed when exhausted nature
consigned the luminous and impassioned Lady St.
Jerome to inevitable silence.   Monsignore Catesby
felt he was bound in honour to make some diversion
in her favour; repeat some of her unanswered in-
quiries, and reiterate some of her unnoticed views;
but the only return he received was silence without
a bow, and then the physician remarked, "I presume
I can now see the patient."

The English physician was alone with Lothair
for some time, and then he met in consultation the
usual attendants.   The result of all these proceedings
was that he returned to the saloon, in which he
found Lord and Lady St. Jerome, Monsignore
Catesby, and Father Coleman, and he then said,
"My opinion is that his Lordship should quit Rome
immediately, and I think he had better return at
once to his own country."

All the efforts of the English Propaganda were
now directed to prevent the return of Lothair to his
own country.   The Cardinal and Lady St. Jerome,
and the Monsignore, and Father Coleman, all the
beautiful young countesses who had 'gone over' to
Rome, and all the spirited young earls who had
come over to bring their wives back, but had unfortunately remained themselves, looked very serious,
and spoke much in whispers.   Lord St. Jerome was
firm that Lothair should immediately leave the city,

and find that change of scene and air which were
declared by authority to be indispensable for his
health, both of mind and body. But his return to
England, at this moment, was an affair of serious
difficulty. He could not return unattended, and
attended too by some intimate and devoted friend.
Besides it was very doubtful whether Lothair had
strength remaining to bear so great an exertion, and
at such a season of the year—and he seemed disin-
clined to it himself. He also wished to leave Rome,
but he wished also in time to extend his travels.
Amidst these difficulties a Neapolitan duke, a great
friend of Monsignore Catesby, a gentleman who always had a friend in need, offered to the young
English noble, the interesting young Englishman so
favoured by heaven, the use of his villa on the coast
of the remotest part of Sicily, near Syracuse. Here
was a solution of many difficulties; departure from
Rome, change of scene and air—sea air, too, particularly recommended—and almost the same as a
return to England, without an effort, for was it not
an island, only with a better climate, and a people
with free institutions, or a taste for them, which is
the same?

The mode in which Lady St. Jerome and Monsignore Catesby consulted Lord St. Jerome on the
subject, took the adroit but insidious form of congratulating him on the entire and unexpected fulfilment
of his purpose. "Are we not fortunate?" exclaimed
her Ladyship, looking up brightly in his face, and
gently pressing one of his arms.

"Exactly everything your Lordship required,"

echoed Monsignore Catesby, congratulating him by pressing the other.

The Cardinal said to Lord St. Jerome in the course of the morning, in an easy way, and as if he were not thinking too much of the matter, "So you have got out of all your difficulties."

Lord St. Jerome was not entirely satisfied, but he thought he had done a great deal, and, to say the truth, the effort for him had not been inconsiderable; and so the result was that Lothair, accompanied by Monsignore Catesby and Father Coleman, travelled by easy stages, and chiefly on horseback, through a delicious and romantic country, which alone did Lothair a great deal of good, to the coast; crossed the straits on a serene afternoon, visited Messina and Palermo, and finally settled at their point of destination—the Villa Catalano.

Nothing could be more satisfactory than the Monsignore's bulletin, announcing to his friends at Rome their ultimate arrangement. Three weeks' travel, air, horse exercise, the inspiration of the landscape and the clime, had wonderfully restored Lothair, and they might entirely count on his passing Holy Week at Rome, when all they had hoped and prayed for would, by the blessing of the Holy Virgin, be accomplished.

CHAPTER XXV.

THE terrace of the Villa Catalano, with its orange and palm trees, looked upon a sea of lapis lazuli, and rose from a shelving shore of aloes and arbutus. The waters reflected the colour of the sky, and all the foliage was bedewed with the same violet light of morn which bathed the softness of the distant mountains, and the undulating beauty of the ever-varying coast.

Lothair was walking on the terrace, his favourite walk, for it was the only occasion on which he ever found himself alone. Not that he had any reason to complain of his companions. More complete ones could scarcely be selected. Travel which, they say, tries all tempers, had only proved the engaging equanimity of Catesby, and had never disturbed the amiable repose of his brother priest: and then they were so entertaining and so instructive, as well as handy and experienced in all common things. The Monsignore had so much taste and feeling and various knowledge; and as for the reverend Father, all the antiquaries they daily encountered were mere children in his hands who, without effort, could explain and illustrate every scene and object, and spoke as if he had never given a thought to any other theme than Sicily and Syracuse, the expedition of Nicias and the adventures of Agathocles. And

yet during all their travels Lothair felt that he never
was alone. This was remarkable at the great cities
such as Messina and Palermo, but it was a prevalent
habit in less frequented places. There was a petty
town near them, which he had never visited alone,
although he had made more than one attempt with
that view; and it was only on the terrace in the
early morn, a spot whence he could be observed
from the villa, and which did not easily communicate with the precipitous and surrounding scenery,
that Lothair would indulge that habit of introspection
which he had pursued through many a long ride,
and which to him was a never-failing source of interest and even excitement.

He wanted to ascertain the causes of what he
deemed the failure of his life, and of the dangers
and discomfiture that were still impending over him.
Were these causes to be found in any peculiarity of
his disposition, or in the general inexperience and
incompetence of youth? The latter he was now
quite willing to believe would lead their possessors
into any amount of disaster, but his ingenuous
nature hesitated before it accepted them as the self-
complacent solution of his present deplorable position.

Of a nature profound and inquisitive, though
with a great fund of reverence which had been developed by an ecclesiastical education, Lothair now
felt that he had started in life with an extravagant
appreciation of the influence of the religious principle on the conduct of human affairs. With him,
when heaven was so nigh, earth could not be re-

membered; and yet experience showed, that so long
as one was on the earth, the incidents of this planet
considerably controlled one's existence, both in be-
haviour and in thought.   All the world could not
retire to Mount Athos.   It was clear, therefore, that
there was a juster conception of the relations between religion and life than that which he had at
first adopted.

Practically, Theodora had led, or was leading,
him to this result; but Theodora, though religious,
did not bow before those altars to which he for a
moment had never been faithless.   Theodora believed in her immortality, and did not believe in
death according to the ecclesiastical interpretation.
But her departure from the scene, and the circumstances under which it had taken place, had unexpectedly and violently restored the course of his life
to its old bent. Shattered and shorn, he was willing
to believe that he was again entering the kingdom
of heaven, but found he was only under the gilded
dome of a Jesuit's church, and woke to reality, from
a scene of magical deceptions, with a sad conviction
that even cardinals and fathers of the Church were
inevitably influenced in this life by its interests and
its passions.

But the incident of his life that most occupied—
it might be said engrossed—his meditation was the
midnight apparition in the Coliseum.   Making every
allowance that a candid nature and an ingenious
mind could suggest for explicatory circumstances;
the tension of his nervous system, which was then
doubtless strained to its last point; the memory of

her death-scene which always harrowed and haunted
him; and that dark collision between his promise
and his life which then, after so many efforts, appeared by some supernatural ordination to be about
inevitably to occur in that very Rome whose gigantic
shades surrounded him; he still could not resist the
conviction that he had seen the form of Theodora
and had listened to her voice. Often the whole day
when they were travelling, and his companions
watched him on his saddle in silent thought, his
mind In reality was fixed on this single incident,
and he was cross-examining his memory as some
adroit and ruthless advocate deals with the witness
in the box, and tries to demonstrate his infidelity or
his weakness.

But whether it were indeed the apparition of his
adored friend or a distempered dream, Lothair not
less recognised the warning as divine, and the only
conviction he had arrived at throughout his Sicilian
travels was a determination that, however tragical the
cost, his promise to Theodora should never be
broken.

The beautiful terrace of the Villa Catalano over-
looked a small bay to which it descended by winding walks. The water was deep, and in any other
country the bay might have been turned to good account, but bays abounded on this coast, and the
people, with many harbours, had no freights to occupy them. This morn, this violet morn, when the
balm of the soft breeze refreshed Lothair, and the
splendour of the rising sun began to throw a flashing line upon the azure waters, a few fishermen in

one of the country boats happened to come in, about to dry a net upon a sunny bank. The boat was what is called a speronaro; an open boat worked with oars, but with a lateen sail at the same time when the breeze served.

Lothair admired the trim of the vessel, and got talking with the men as they eat their bread and olives, and a small fish or two.

"And your lateen sail—?" continued Lothair.

"Is the best thing in the world, except in a white squall," replied the sailor, "and then everything is queer in these seas with an open boat, though I am not afraid of Santa Agnese, and that is her name. But I took two English officers who came over here for sport, and whose leave of absence was out,—I took them over in her to Malta, and did it in ten hours. I believe it had never been done in an open boat before, but it was neck or nothing with them."

"And you saved them?"

"With the lateen up the whole way."

"They owed you much, and I hope they paid you well."

"I asked them ten ducats," said the man, "and they paid me ten ducats."

Lothair had his hand in his pocket all this time, feeling, but imperceptibly, for his purse, and when he had found it, feeling how it was lined. He generally carried about him as much as Fortunatus.

"What are you going to do with yourselves this morning?" said Lothair.

"Well, not much; we thought of throwing the net, but we have had one dip, and no great luck."

"Are you inclined to give me a sail?"

"Certainly, signor."

"Have you a mind to go to Malta?"

"That is business, signor."

"Look here," said Lothair, "here are ten ducats in this purse, and a little more. I will give them to you if you will take me to Malta at once, but if you will start in a hundred seconds, before the sun touches that rock, and the waves just beyond it are already bright, you shall have ten more ducats when you reach the isle."

"Step in, signor."

From the nature of the course, which was not in the direction of the open sea, for they had to double Cape Passaro, the speronaro was out of the sight of the villa in a few minutes. They rowed only till they had doubled the cape, and then set the lateen sail, the breeze being light but steady and favourable. They were soon in open sea, no land in sight. "And if a white squall does rise," thought Lothair, "it will only settle many difficulties."

But no white squall came; everything was favourable to their progress; the wind, the current, the courage and spirit of the men, who liked the adventure and liked Lothair. Night came on, but they were as tender to him as women, fed him with their least coarse food, and covered him with a cloak made of stuff spun by their mothers and their sisters.

Lothair was slumbering when the patron of the boat roused him, and he saw at hand many lights, and in a few minutes was in still water. They were in one of the harbours of Malta, but not permitted to land at midnight, and when the morn arrived, the obstacles to the release of Lothair were not easily removed. A speronaro, an open boat from Sicily, of course with no papers to prove their point of departure—here were materials for doubt and difficulty, of which the petty officers of the port knew how to avail themselves. They might come from Barbary, from an infected port; plague might be aboard, a question of quarantine. Lothair observed that they were nearly alongside of a fine steam yacht, English, for it bore the cross of St. George, and while on the quay, he and the patron of the speronaro arguing with the officers of the port, a gentleman from the yacht put ashore in a boat, of which the bright equipment immediately attracted attention. The gentleman landed almost close to the point where the controversy was carrying on. The excited manner and voice of the Sicilian mariner could not escape notice. The gentleman stopped and looked at the group, and then suddenly exclaimed, "Good heavens! my Lord, can it be you?"

"Ah! Mr. Phœbus, you will help me," said Lothair, and then he went up to him and told him everything. All difficulties of course vanished before the presence of Mr. Phœbus, whom the officers of the port evidently looked upon as a being beyond criticism and control.

"And now," said Mr. Phœbus, "about your people and your baggage."

"I have neither servants nor clothes," said Lothair, "and if it had not been for these good people, I should not have had food."

CHAPTER XXVI.

Mr. Phœnus in his steam-yacht Pan, of considerable admeasurement and fitted up with every luxury and convenience that science and experience could suggest, was on his way to an island which he occasionally inhabited, near the Asian coast of the Ægean Sea, and which he rented from the chief of his wife's house, the Prince of Samos. Mr. Phœbus, by his genius and fame, commanded a large income, and he spent it freely and fully. There was nothing of which he more disapproved than accumulation. It was a practice which led to sordid habits and was fatal to the beautiful. On the whole, he thought it more odious even than debt, more permanently degrading. Mr. Phœbus liked pomp and graceful ceremony, and he was of opinion that great artists should lead a princely life, so that in their manners and method of existence they might furnish models to mankind in general, and elevate the tone and taste of nations.

Sometimes when he observed a friend noticing with admiration, perhaps with astonishment, the splendour or finish of his equipments, he would say,

"The world think I had a large fortune with Madame
Phœbus. I had nothing. I understand that a fortune, and no inconsiderable one, would have been
given, had I chosen to ask for it. But I did not
choose to ask for it. I made Madame Phœbus my
wife because she was the finest specimen of the
Aryan race that I was acquainted with, and I would
have no considerations mixed up with the high
motive that influenced me. My father-in-law Cantacuzene, whether from a feeling of gratitude or
remorse, is always making us magnificent presents.
I like to receive magnificent presents, but also to
make them; and I presented him with a picture
which is the gem of his gallery, and which, if he
ever part with it, will in another generation be con-
tended for by kings and peoples.

"On her last birthday we breakfasted with my
father-in-law Cantacuzene, and Madame Phœbus
found in her napkin a cheque for five thousand
pounds. I expended it immediately in jewels for
her personal use; for I wished my father-in-law to
understand that there are other princely families in
the world besides the Cantacuzenes."

A friend once ventured enquiringly to suggest
whether his way of life might not be conducive to
envy and so disturb that serenity of sentiment necessary to the complete life of an artist. But Mr. Phœbus would not for a moment admit the soundness
of the objection. "No," he said, "envy is a purely
intellectual process. Splendour never excites it; a
man of splendour is looked upon always with favour
—his appearance exhilarates the heart of man. He

is always popular. People wish to dine with him,
to borrow his money, but they do not envy him. If
you want to know what envy is you should live
among artists. You should hear me lecture at the
Academy. I have sometimes suddenly turned round
and caught countenances like that of the man who
was waiting at the corner of the street for Benvenuto
Cellini, in order to assassinate the great Florentine."

It was impossible for Lothair in his present condition to have fallen upon a more suitable companion
than Mr. Phœbus. It is not merely change of scene
and air that we sometimes want, but a revolution in
the atmosphere of thought and feeling in which we
live and breathe. Besides his great intelligence and
fancy, and his peculiar views on art and man and
affairs in general, which always interested their
bearer and sometimes convinced, there was a general
vivacity in Mr. Phœbus and a vigorous sense of life
which were inspiriting to his companions. When
there was anything to be done, great or small, Mr.
Phœbus liked to do it; and this, as he averred, from
a sense of duty, since, if anything is to be done, it
should be done in the best manner, and no one
could do it so well as Mr. Phœbus. He always
acted as if he had been created to be the oracle
and model of the human race, but the oracle was
never pompous or solemn, and the model was always
beaming with good nature and high spirits.

Mr. Phœbus liked Lothair. He liked youth, and
good-looking youth; and youth that was intelligent
and engaging and well-mannered. He also liked
old men. But between fifty and seventy, he saw

little to approve of in the dark sex. They had lost their good looks if they ever had any, their wits were on the wane, and they were invariably selfish. When they attained second childhood the charm often returned. Age was frequently beautiful, wisdom appeared like an aftermath, and the heart which seemed dry and deadened suddenly put forth shoots of sympathy.

Mr. Phœbus postponed his voyage in order that Lothair might make his preparations to become his guest in his island. "I cannot take you to a banker," said Mr. Phœbus, "for I have none; but I wish you would share my purse. Nothing will ever induce me to use what they call paper money. It is the worst thing that what they call civilisation has produced; neither hue nor shape, and yet a substitute for the richest colour, and, where the arts flourish, the finest forms."

The telegraph which brought an order to the bankers at Malta to give an unlimited credit to Lothair, rendered it unnecessary for our friend to share what Mr. Phœbus called his purse, and yet he was glad to have the opportunity of seeing it, as Mr. Phœbus one morning opened a chest in his cabin and produced several velvet bags, one full of pearls, another of rubies, others of Venetian sequins, Napoleons, and golden piastres. "I like to look at them," said Mr. Phœbus, "and find life more intense when they are about my person. But bank notes, so cold and thin—they give me an ague."

Madame Phœbus and her sister Euphrosyne welcomed Lothair in maritime costumes which were ab-

solutely bewitching; wondrous jackets with loops of
pearls, girdles defended by dirks with handles of
turquoises, and tilted hats that, while they screened
their long eyelashes from the sun, crowned the
longer braids of their never ending hair. Mr. Phœbus gave banquets every day on board his yacht,
attended by the chief personages of the island and
the most agreeable officers of the garrison. They
dined upon deck, and it delighted him, with a sur-
face of sangfroid, to produce a repast which both in
its material and its treatment was equal to the
refined festivals of Paris. Sometimes they had a
dance; sometimes in his barge, rowed by a crew in
Venetian dresses, his guests glided on the tranquil
waters, under a starry sky, and listened to the exquisite melodies of their hostess and her sister.

At length the day of departure arrived. It was
bright, with a breeze favourable to the sail and op-
portune for the occasion. For all the officers of the
garrison and all beautiful Valetta itself seemed
present in their yachts and barges to pay their
last tribute of admiration to the enchanting sisters
and the all-accomplished owner of the "Pan."
Placed on the gallery of his yacht, Mr. Phœbus surveyed the brilliant and animated scene with delight.
"This is the way to conduct life," he said. "If,
fortunately for them, I could have passed another
month among these people, I could have developed
a feeling equal to the old regattas of the Vene-
tians."

The Ægean isle occupied by Mr. Phœbus was of
no inconsiderable dimensions. A chain of mountains

of white marble intersected it, covered with forests of oak, though in parts precipitous and bare. The lowlands, while they produced some good crops of grain, and even cotton and silk, were chiefly clothed with fruit trees: orange and lemon, and the fig, the olive, and the vine. Sometimes the land was uncultivated, and was principally covered with myrtles of large size and oleanders and arbutus and thorny brooms. Here game abounded, while from the mountain forests the wolf sometimes descended and spoiled and scared the islanders.

On the seashore, yet not too near the wave, and on a sylvan declivity, was a long pavilion-looking building, painted in white and arabesque. It was backed by the forest, which had a park-like character from its partial clearance, and which, after a convenient slip of even land, ascended the steeper country and took the form of wooded hills, backed in due time by still sylvan yet loftier elevations, and sometimes a glittering peak.

"Welcome, my friend!" said Mr. Phœbus to Lothair. "Welcome to an Aryan clime, an Aryan landscape, and an Aryan race. It will do you good after your Semitic hallucinations."

CHAPTER XXVII.

MR. PHŒBUS pursued a life in his island partly feudal, partly oriental, partly Venetian, and partly idiosyncratic. He had a grand studio where he could always find interesting occupation in drawing every fine face and form in his dominions. Then he hunted, and that was a remarkable scene. The ladies, looking like Diana or her nymphs, were mounted on cream-coloured Anatolian chargers with golden bells; while Mr. Phœbus himself, in green velvet and seven-leagued boots, sounded a wondrous twisted horn rife with all the inspiring or directing notes of musical and learned venerie. His neighbours of condition came mounted, but the field was by no means confined to cavaliers. A vast crowd of men in small caps and jackets and huge white breeches, and armed with all the weapons of Palikari, handjars and yataghans and silver sheathed muskets of uncommon length and almost as old as the battle of Lepanto, always rallied round his standard. The equestrians caracolled about the park, and the horns sounded and the hounds bayed and the men shouted till the deer had all scudded away. Then, by degrees, the hunters entered the forest, and the notes of venerie became more faint and the shouts more distant. Then for two or three hours all was silent, save the sound of an occasional shot or the note of a stray hound, until the human stragglers began to reappear emerging from the forest, and in due time the great body of the hunt, and a gilded cart drawn by mules and carrying the prostrate forms of fallow deer and roebuck. None of the ceremonies of the chase were omitted, and the crowd dispersed, refreshed by Samian wine, which Mr. Phœbus was teaching them to make without resin, and which they quaffed with shrugging shoulders.

"We must have a wolf-hunt for you," said Euphrosyne to Lothair. "You like excitement, I believe?"

"Well, I am rather inclined for repose at present, and I came here with the hope of obtaining it."

"Well, we are never idle here; in fact that would be impossible with Gaston. He has established here an academy of the fine arts and also revived the gymnasia; and my sister and myself have schools—only music and dancing; Gaston does not approve of letters. The poor people have of course their primary schools with their priests, and Gaston does not interfere with them, but he regrets their existence. He looks upon reading and writing as very injurious to education."

Sometimes reposing on divans, the sisters received the chief persons of the isle, and regaled them with fruits and sweetmeats and coffee and sherbets, while Gaston's chibouques and tobacco of Salonica were a proverb. These meetings always ended with dance and song, replete, according to Mr. Phœbus, with studies of Aryan life.

"I believe these islanders to be an unmixed

race," said Mr. Phœbus. "The same form and
visage prevails throughout; and very little changed
in anything—even in their religion."

"Unchanged in their religion!" said Lothair with
some astonishment.

"Yes; you will find it so. Their existence is
easy; their wants are not great, and their means of
subsistence plentiful. They pass much of their life
in what is called amusement—and what is it? They
make parties of pleasure; they go in procession to a
fountain or a grove. They dance and eat fruit, and
they return home singing songs. They have, in fact,
been performing unconsciously the religious ceremonies of their ancestors, and which they pursue,
and will for ever, though they may have forgotten
the name of the dryad or the nymph who presides
over their waters."

"I should think their priests would guard them
from these errors," said Lothair.

"The Greek priests, particularly in these Asian
islands, are good sort of people," said Mr. Phœbus.
"They marry and have generally large families, often
very beautiful. They have no sacerdotal feelings,
for they never can have any preferment; all the high
posts in the Greek Church being reserved for the
monks, who study what is called theology. The
Greek parish priest is not at all Semitic; there is
nothing to counteract his Aryan tendencies. I have
already raised the statue of a nymph at one of their
favourite springs and places of pleasant pilgrimage,
and I have a statue now in the island, still in its
case, which I contemplate installing in a famous

grove of laurel not far off and very much resorted
to."

"And what then?" enquired Lothair.

"Well, I have a conviction that among the great
races the old creeds will come back," said Mr.
Phœbus, "and it will be acknowledged that true religion is the worship of the beautiful. For the beautiful cannot be attained without virtue, if virtue consists, as I believe, in the control of the passions, in
the sentiment of repose, and the avoidance in all
things of excess."

One night Lothair was walking home with the
sisters from a village festival, where they had been
much amused.

"You have had a great many adventures since
we first met?" said Madame Phœbus.

"Which makes it seem longer ago than it really
is," said Lothair.

"You count time by emotion then?" said Euphrosyne.

"Well, it is a wonderful thing however it be com-
puted," said Lothair.

"For my part, I do not think that it ought to be
counted at all," said Madame Phœbus; "and there
is nothing to me so detestable in Europe as the
quantity of clocks and watches."

"Do you use a watch, my Lord?" asked Euphrosyne in a tone which always seemed to Lothair
one of mocking artlessness.

"I believe I never wound it up when I had one,"
said Lothair.

"But you make such good use of your time,"
said Madame Phœbus, "you do not require watches."

"I am glad to hear I make good use of my time,"
said Lothair, but a little surprised.

"But you are so good, so religious," said Madame
Phœbus. "That is a great thing; especially for one
so young."

"Hem!" said Lothair.

"That must have been a beautiful procession at
Rome," said Euphrosyne.

"I was rather a spectator of it than an actor in
it," said Lothair with some seriousness. "It is too
long a tale to enter into, but my part in those proceedings was entirely misrepresented."

"I believe that nothing in the newspapers is ever
true," said Madame Phœbus.

"And that is why they are so popular," added
Euphrosyne; "the taste of the age being so decidedly
for fiction."

"Is it true that you escaped from a convent to
Malta?" said Madame Phœbus.

"Not quite," said Lothair, "but true enough for
conversation."

"As confidential as the present, I suppose?" said
Euphrosyne.

"Yes, when we are grave, as we are inclined to
be now," said Lothair.

"Then, you have been fighting a good deal,"
said Madame Phœbus.

"You are putting me on a court martial, Madame
Phœbus," said Lothair.

"But we do not know on which side you were," said Euphrosyne.

"That is matter of history," said Lothair, "and that, you know, is always doubtful."

"Well, I do not like fighting," said Madame Phœbus, "and for my part I never could find out that it did any good."

"And what do you like?" said Lothair. "Tell me how would you pass your life?"

"Well, much as I do. I do not know that I want any change, except I think I should like it to be always summer."

"And I would have perpetual spring," said Euphrosyne.

"But, summer or spring, what would be your favourite pursuit?"

"Well, dancing is very nice," said Madame Phœbus.

"But we cannot always be dancing," said Lothair.

"Then we would sing," said Euphrosyne.

"But the time comes when one can neither dance nor sing," said Lothair.

"Oh! then we become part of the audience," said Madame Phœbus, "the people for whose amusement everybody labours."

"And enjoy power without responsibility," said Euphrosyne, "detect false notes and mark awkward gestures. How can anyone doubt of Providence with such a system of constant compensation!"

There was something in the society of these two sisters that Lothair began to find highly attractive.

Their extraordinary beauty, their genuine and unflagging gaiety, their thorough enjoyment of existence,
and the variety of resources with which they made
life amusing and graceful, all contributed to captivate
him. They had, too, a great love and knowledge
both of art and nature, and insensibly they weaned
Lothair from that habit of introspection which, though
natural to him, he had too much indulged, and
taught him to find sources of interest and delight in
external objects. He was beginning to feel happy
in this island, and wishing that his life might never
change, when one day Mr. Phœbus informed them
that the Prince Agathonides, the eldest son of the
Prince of Samos, would arrive from Constantinople
in a few days, and would pay them a visit. "He
will come with some retinue," said Mr. Phœbus,
"but I trust we shall be able by our reception to
show that the Cantacuzenes are not the only princely
family in the world."

Mr. Phœbus was confident in his resources in
this respect, for his yacht's crew in their Venetian
dresses could always furnish a guard of honour which
no Grecian prince or Turkish pacha could easily
rival. When the eventful day arrived he was quite
equal to the occasion. The yacht was dressed in
every part with the streaming colours of all nations,
the banner of Gaston Phœbus waved from his
pavilion, the guard of honour kept the ground, but
the population of the isle were present in numbers
and in their most showy costume, and a battery of
ancient Turkish guns fired a salute without an ac-
cident.

The Prince Agathonides was a youth, good-looking and dressed in a splendid Palikar costume, though his manners were quite European, being an attaché to the Turkish embassy at Vienna. He had with him a sort of governor, a secretary, servants in Mamlouk dresses, pipe-bearers, and grooms, there being some horses as presents from his father to Mr. Phœbus, and some rarely embroidered kerchiefs and choice perfumes and Persian greyhounds for the ladies.

The arrival of the young Prince was the signal for a series of entertainments in the island. First of all Mr. Phœbus resolved to give a dinner in the Frank style, to prove to Agathonides that there were other members of the Cantacuzene family besides himself who comprehended a firstrate Frank dinner. The chief people of the island were invited to this banquet. They drank the choicest grapes of France and Germany, were stuffed with truffles, and sate on little cane chairs. But one might detect in their countenances how they sighed for their easy divans, their simple dishes, and their resinous wine. Then there was a wolf hunt, and other sport; a great day of gymnasia, many dances and much music; in fact, there were choruses all over the island, and every night was a serenade.

Why such general joy? Because it was understood that the heir apparent of the isle, their future sovereign, had in fact arrived to make his bow to the beautiful Euphrosyne, though he saw her for the first time.

CHAPTER XXVIII.

VERY shortly after his arrival at Malta, Mr.
Phœbus had spoken to Lothair about Theodora. It
appeared that Lucien Campian, though severely
wounded, had escaped with Garibaldi after the battle
of Mentana into the Italian territories. Here they
were at once arrested, but not severely detained,
and Colonel Campian took the first opportunity of
revisiting England, where, after settling his affairs,
he had returned to his native country, from which
he had been separated for many years. Mr. Phœbus
during the interval had seen a great deal of him,
and the Colonel departed for America under the impression that Lothair had been among the slain at
the final struggle.

"Campian is one of the best men I ever knew,"
said Phœbus. "He was a remarkable instance of
energy combined with softness of disposition. In
my opinion, however, he ought never to have visited
Europe: he was made to clear the back woods, and
govern man by the power of his hatchet and the
mildness of his words. He was fighting for freedom
all his life, yet slavery made and slavery destroyed
him. Among all the freaks of fate nothing is more
surprising than that this Transatlantic planter should
have been ordained to be the husband of a divine
being—a true Hellenic goddess, who in the good

days would have been worshipped in this country
and have inspired her race to actions of grace, wisdom, and beauty."

"I greatly esteem him," said Lothair, "and I
shall write to him directly."

"Except by Campian, who spoke probably about
you to no one save myself," continued Phœbus,
"your name has never been mentioned with reference
to those strange transactions. Once there was a
sort of rumour that you had met with some mishap,
but these things were contradicted and explained,
and then forgotten: and people were all out of town.
I believe that Cardinal Grandison communicated with
your man of business, and between them everything
was kept quiet, until this portentous account of your
doings at Rome, which transpired after we left England and which met us at Malta."

"I have written to my man of business about
that," said Lothair, "but I think it will tax all his
ingenuity to explain, or to mystify it as successfully
as he did the preceding adventures. At any rate, he
will not have the assistance of my Lord Cardinal."

"Theodora was a remarkable woman on many
accounts," said Mr. Phœbus, "but particularly on
this, that, although one of the most beautiful women
that ever existed, she was adored by beautiful women.
My wife adored her; Euphrosyne, who has no enthusiasm, adored her; the Princess of Tivoli, the
most capricious being probably that ever existed,
adored, and always adored, Theodora. I think it
must have been that there was on her part a total
absence of vanity, and this the more strange in one

whose vocation in her earlier life had been to attract
and live on popular applause; but I have seen her quit
theatres ringing with admiration and enter her carriage with the serenity of a Phidian muse."

"I adored her," said Lothair, "but I never could
quite solve her character. Perhaps it was too rich
and deep for rapid comprehension."

"We shall never perhaps see her like again,"
said Mr. Phœbus. "It was a rare combination, peculiar to the Tyrrhenian sea. I am satisfied that we
must go there to find the pure Hellenic blood, and
from thence it got to Rome."

"We may not see her like again, but we may see
her again," said Lothair; "and sometimes I think
she is always hovering over me."

In this vein, when they were alone, they were
frequently speaking of the departed, and one day—
it was before the arrival of Prince Agathonides—
Mr. Phœbus said to Lothair, "We will ride this
morning to what we call the grove of Daphne. It
is a real laurel grove. Some of the trees must be
immemorial, and deserve to have been sacred, if
once they were not so. In their huge grotesque
forms you would not easily recognise your polished
friends of Europe, so trim and glossy and shrublike.
The people are very fond of this grove and make
frequent processions there. Once a year they must
be headed by their priest. No one knows why, nor
has he the slightest idea of the reason of the various
ceremonies which he that day performs. But we
know, and some day he or his successors will equally
understand them. Yes, if I remain here long enough

—and I sometimes think I will never again quit the isle—I shall expect some fine summer night, when there is that rich stillness which the whispering waves only render more intense, to hear a voice of music on the mountains declaring that the god Pan has returned to earth."

It was a picturesque ride, as every ride was on this island, skirting the sylvan hills with the sea glimmering in the distance. Lothair was pleased with the approaches to the sacred grove: now and then a single tree with grey branches and a green head, then a great spread of underwood, all laurel, and then spontaneous plantations of young trees.

"There was always a vacant space in the centre of the grove," said Mr. Phœbus, "once sadly overrun with wild shrubs, but I have cleared it and restored the genius of the spot. See!"

They entered the sacred circle and beheld a statue raised on a porphyry pedestal. The light fell with magical effect on the face of the statue. It was the statue of Theodora, the placing of which in the pavilion of Belmont Mr. Phœbus was superintending when Lothair first made his acquaintance.

CHAPTER XXIX.

THE Prince Agathonides seemed quite to mono-
polise the attention of Madame Phœbus and her
sister. This was not very unreasonable, considering
that he was their visitor, the future chief of their
house, and had brought them so many embroidered
pocket-handkerchiefs, choice scents and fancy dogs.
But Lothair thought it quite disgusting, nor could
he conceive what they saw in him, what they were
talking about or laughing about, for, so far as he
had been able to form any opinion on the subject,
the Prince was a shallow-pated coxcomb without a
single quality to charm any woman of sense and
spirit. Lothair began to consider how he could pursue his travels, where he should go to, and when
that was settled, how he should get there.

Just at this moment of perplexity, as is often the
case, something occurred which no one could fore-
see, but which like every event removed some difficulties and introduced others.

There arrived at the island a despatch forwarded
to Mr. Phœbus by the Russian Ambassador at Constantinople, who had received it from his colleague
at London. This despatch contained a proposition
to Mr. Phœbus to repair to the Court of St. Peters-
burgh, and accept appointments of high distinction
and emolument. Without in any way restricting the

independent pursuit of his profession, he was offered
a large salary, the post of Court painter, and the
Presidency of the Academy of Fine Arts. Of such
moment did the Russian Government deem the official presence of this illustrious artist in their country,
that it was intimated, if the arrangement could be
effected, its conclusion might be celebrated by conferring on Mr. Phœbus a patent of nobility and a
decoration of a high class. The despatch contained
a private letter from an exalted member of the Imperial family, who had had the high and gratifying
distinction of making Mr. Phœbus's acquaintance in
London, personally pressing the acceptance by him
of the general proposition, assuring him of cordial
welcome and support, and informing Mr. Phœbus
that what was particularly desired at this moment
was a series of paintings illustrative of some of the
most memorable scenes in the Holy Land and especially the arrival of the pilgrims of the Greek rite at
Jerusalem. As for this purpose he would probably
like to visit Palestine, the whole of the autumn or
even a longer period was placed at his disposal, so
that, enriched with all necessary drawings and studies, he might achieve his more elaborate perform-
ances in Russia at his leisure and with every advantage.

Considering that the great objects in life with
Mr. Phœbus were to live in an Aryan country, amid
an Aryan race, and produce works which should revive for the benefit of human nature Aryan creeds,
a proposition to pass some of the prime years of his
life among the Mongolian race, and at the same

time devote his pencil to the celebration of Semitic
subjects, was startling.

"I shall say nothing to Madame Phœbus until
the Prince has gone," he remarked to Lothair: "he
will go the day after to-morrow. I do not know
what they may offer to make me—probably only a
Baron, perhaps a Count. But you know in Russia
a man may become a Prince, and I certainly should
like those Cantacuzenes to feel that after all their
daughter is a Princess with no thanks to them. The
climate is detestable, but one owes much to one's
profession. Art would be honoured at a great, perhaps the greatest, Court. There would not be a
fellow at his easel in the streets about Fitzroy Square
who would not be prouder. I wonder what the decoration will be. 'Of a high class'—vague. It might
be Alexander Newsky. You know you have a right,
whatever your decoration, to have it expressed, of
course at your own expense, in brilliants. I confess
I have my weaknesses. I should like to get over to
the Academy dinner—one can do anything in these
days of railroads—and dine with the R. A.s in my
ribbon and the star of the Alexander Newsky in
brilliants. I think every Academician would feel
elevated. What I detest are their Semitic subjects—
nothing but drapery. They cover even their heads
in those scorching climes. Can anyone make anything of a caravan of pilgrims? To be sure, they say
no one can draw a camel. If I went to Jerusalem
a camel would at last be drawn. There is something in that. We must think over these things, and
when the Prince has gone talk it over with Madame

Phœbus. I wish you all to come to a wise decision, without the slightest reference to my individual tastes or, it may be, prejudices."

The result of all this was that Mr. Phœbus, without absolutely committing himself, favourably entertained the general proposition of the Russian Court; while, with respect to their particular object in art, he agreed to visit Palestine and execute at least one work for his Imperial friend and patron. He counted on reaching Jerusalem before the Easter pilgrims returned to their homes.

"If they would make me a Prince at once and give me the Alexander Newsky in brilliants it might be worth thinking of," he said to Lothair.

The ladies, though they loved their isle, were quite delighted with the thought of going to Jerusalem. Madame Phœbus knew a Russian Grand Duchess who had boasted to her that she had been both to Jerusalem and Torquay, and Madame Phœbus had felt quite ashamed that she had been to neither.

"I suppose you will feel quite at home there," said Euphrosyne to Lothair.

"No; I never was there."

"No; but you know all about those places and people—holy places and holy persons. The Blessed Virgin did not, I believe, appear to you. It was to a young lady, was it not? We were asking each other last night who the young lady could be."

CHAPTER XXX.

TIME, which changes everything, is changing even the traditionary appearance of forlorn Jerusalem. Not that its mien, after all, was ever very sad. Its airy site, its splendid mosque, its vast monasteries, the bright material of which the whole city is built, its cupolaed houses of freestone, and above all the towers and gates and battlements of its lofty and complete walls, always rendered it a handsome city. Jerusalem has not been sacked so often or so recently as the other two great ancient cities, Rome and Athens. Its vicinage was never more desolate than the Campagna, or the state of Attica and the Morea in 1830.

The battlefield of western Asia from the days of the Assyrian kings to those of Mehemet Ali, Palestine endured the same devastation as in modern times has been the doom of Flanders and the Milanese; but the years of havoc in the Low Countries and Lombardy must be counted in Palestine by centuries. Yet the wide plains of the Holy Land, Sharon and Shechem and Esdraelon, have recovered; they are as fertile and as fair as in old days; it is the hill culture that has been destroyed, and that is the culture on which Jerusalem mainly depended. Its hills were terraced gardens, vineyards, and groves of olive trees. And here it is that we find renova-

tion. The terraces are again ascending the stony
heights, and the eye is frequently gladdened with
young plantations. Fruit trees, the peach and the
pomegranate, the almond and the fig, offer gracious
groups; and the true children of the land, the vine
and the olive, are again exulting in their native
soil.

There is óne spot, however, which has been neglected, and yet the one that should have been the
first remembered, as it has been the most rudely
wasted. Blessed be the hand which plants trees
upon Olivet! Blessed be the hand that builds gardens about Sion!

The most remarkable creation, however, in
modern Jerusalem is the Russian settlement which
within a few years has risen on the elevated ground
on the western side of the city. The Latin, the
Greek, and the Armenian Churches had for centuries
possessed enclosed establishments in the city, which,
under the name of monasteries, provided shelter and
protection for hundreds—it might be said even thousands—of pilgrims belonging to their respective rites.
The great scale, therefore, on which Russia secured
hospitality for her subjects was not in reality so
remarkable as the fact that it seemed to indicate a
settled determination to separate the Muscovite
Church altogether from the Greek, and throw off
what little dependence is still acknowledged on the
Patriarchate of Constantinople. Whatever the motive,
the design has been accomplished on a large scale.
The Russian buildings, all well defended, are a cara-
vanserai, a cathedral, a citadel. The consular flag

crowns the height and indicates the office of administration; priests and monks are permanent inhabitants, and a whole caravan of Muscovite pilgrims and the trades on which they depend can be accommodated within the precinct.

Mr. Phœbus, his family and suite were to be the guests of the Russian Consul, and every preparation was made to insure the celebrated painter a becoming reception. Frequent telegrams had duly impressed the representative of all the Russias in the Holy Land with the importance of his impending visitor. Even the qualified and strictly provisional acceptance of the Russian proposition by Mr. Phœbus had agitated the wires of Europe scarcely less than a suggested Conference.

"An artist should always remember what he owes to posterity and his profession," said Mr. Phœbus to Lothair, as they were walking the deck, "even if you can distinguish between them, which I doubt, for it is only by a sense of the beautiful that the human family can be sustained in its proper place in the scale of creation, and the sense of the beautiful is a result of the study of the fine arts. It would be something to sow the seeds of organic change in the Mongolian type, but I am not sanguine of success. There is no original fund of aptitude to act upon. The most ancient of existing communities is Turanian, and yet though they could invent gunpowder and the mariner's compass, they never could understand perspective. Man a-head there! tell Madame Phœbus to come on deck for the first sight of Mount Lebanon."

When the "Pan" entered the port of Joppa they observed another English yacht in those waters; but before they could speculate on its owner they were involved in all the complications of landing. On the quay, the Russian Vice-Consul was in attendance with horses and mules, and donkeys handsomer than either.   The ladies were delighted with the vast orange gardens of Joppa, which Madame Phœbus said realised quite her idea of the Holy Land.

"I was prepared for milk and honey," said Euphrosyne, "but this is too delightful," as she travelled through lanes of date-bearing palm-trees, and sniffed with her almond-shaped nostrils the all-pervading fragrance.

They passed the night at Arimathea, a pretty village surrounded with gardens enclosed with hedges of prickly pear. Here they found hospitality in an old convent, but all the comforts of Europe and many of the refinements of Asia had been forwarded for their accommodation.

"It is a great homage to art," said Mr. Phœbus, as he scattered his gold like a great seigneur of Gascony.

The next day, two miles from Jerusalem, the Consul met them with a cavalcade, and the ladies assured their host that they were not at all wearied with their journey, but were quite prepared, in due time, to join his dinner party, which he was most anxious they should attend, as he had "two English lords" who had arrived, and whom he had invited to meet them. They were all curious to know their names, though that, unfortunately, the Consul could

not tell them, but he had sent to the English Consulate to have them written down. All he could
assure them was that they were real English lords,
not travelling English lords, but in sober earnestness
great personages.

Mr. Phœbus was highly gratified. He was pleased
with his reception. There was nothing he liked much
more than a procession. He was also a sincere
admirer of the aristocracy of his country. "On the
whole," he would say, "they most resemble the old
Hellenic race; excelling in athletic sports, speaking
no other language than their own, and never reading."

"Your fault," he would sometimes say to Lothair,
"and the cause of many of your sorrows, is the
habit of mental introspection. Man is born to observe, but if he falls into psychology he observes
nothing, and then he is astonished that life has no
charms for him, or that, never seizing the occasion,
his career is a failure. No, sir, it is the eye that
must be occupied and cultivated; no one knows the
capacity of the eye who has not developed it, or the
visions of beauty and delight and inexhaustible interest which it commands. To a man who observes,
life is as different as the existence of a dreaming
psychologist is to that of the animals of the field."

"I fear," said Lothair, "that I have at length
found out the truth, and that I am a dreaming psychologist."

"You are young and not irremediably lost," said
Mr. Phœbus. "Fortunately you have received the
admirable though partial education of your class.

You are a good shot, you can ride, you can row,
you can swim. That imperfect secretion of the brain
which is called thought has not yet bowed your
frame. You have not had time to read much. Give
it up altogether. The conversation of a woman like
Theodora is worth all the libraries in the world. If
it were only for her sake, I should wish to save you,
but I wish to do it for your own. Yes, profit by
the vast though calamitous experience which you
have gained in a short time. We may know a great
deal about our bodies, we can know very little about
our minds."

The "real English lords" turned out to be Bertram and St. Aldegonde returning from Nubia. They
had left England about the same time as Lothair,
and had paired together on the Irish Church till
Easter, with a sort of secret hope on the part of
St. Aldegonde that they might neither of them reappear in the House of Commons again until the Irish
Church were either saved or subverted. Holy Week
had long passed, and they were at Jerusalem, not
quite so near the House of Commons as the Reform
Club or the Carlton, but still St. Aldegonde had
mentioned that he was beginning to be bored with
Jerusalem, and Bertram counted on their immediate
departure when they accepted the invitation to dine
with the Russian Consul.

Lothair was unaffectedly delighted to meet Bertram and glad to see St. Aldegonde, but he was a
little nervous and embarrassed as to the probable
tone of his reception by them. But their manner re-

lieved him in an instant, for he saw they knew nothing of his adventures.

"Well," said St. Aldegonde, "what have you been doing with yourself since we last met? I wish you had come with us and had a shot at a crocodile."

Bertram told Lothair in the course of the evening that he found letters at Cairo from Corisande, on his return, in which there was a good deal about Lothair, and which had made him rather uneasy. "That there was a rumour you had been badly wounded, and some other things," and Bertram looked him full in the face; "but I dare say not a word of truth."

"I was never better in my life," said Lothair, "and I have been in Sicily and in Greece. However, we will talk over all this another time."

The dinner at the Consulate was one of the most successful banquets that was ever given, if to please your guests be the test of good fortune in such enterprises. St. Aldegonde was perfectly charmed with the Phœbus family; he did not know which to admire most—the great artist, who was in remarkable spirits to-day, considering he was in a Semitic country, or his radiant wife, or his brilliant sister-in-law. St. Aldegonde took an early opportunity of informing Bertram that if he liked to go over and vote for the Irish Church he would release him from his pair with the greatest pleasure, but for his part he had not the slightest intention of leaving Jerusalem at present. Strange to say, Bertram received this intimation without a murmur. He was not so

loud in his admiration of the Phœbus family as St.
Aldegonde, but there is a silent sentiment sometimes
more expressive than the noisiest applause, and more
dangerous. Bertram had sat next to Euphrosyne
and was entirely spell-bound.

The Consul's wife, a hostess not unworthy of
such guests, had entertained her friends in the European style. The dinner-hour was not late, and the
gentlemen who attended the ladies from the dinner-
table were allowed to remain some time in the
saloon. Lothair talked much to the Consul's wife,
by whose side sat Madame Phœbus. St. Aldegonde
was always on his legs, distracted by the rival attrac-
tions of that lady and her husband. More remote,
Bertram whispered to Euphrosyne, who answered
him with laughing eyes.

At a certain hour, the Consul, attended by his
male guests, crossing a court, proceeded to his divan,
a lofty and capacious chamber painted in fresco,
and with no furniture except the low but broad
raised seat that surrounded the room. Here, when
they were seated, an equal number of attendants—
Arabs in Arab dress, blue gowns and red slippers
and red caps—entered, each proffering a long pipe
of cherry or jasmine wood. Then in a short time
guests dropped in, and pipes and coffee were immediately brought to them. Any person who had been
formally presented to the Consul had this privilege,
without any further invitation. The society often
found in these consular divans in the more remote
places of the east—Cairo, Damascus, Jerusalem—is
often extremely entertaining and instructive. Cele-

brated travellers, distinguished men of science, artists, adventurers who ultimately turn out to be heroes, eccentric characters of all kinds, are here encountered, and give the fruits of their original or experienced observation without reserve.

"It is the smoking-room over again," whispered St. Aldegonde to Lothair, "only in England one is so glad to get away from the women, but here I must say I should have liked to remain behind."

An individual in a Syrian dress, fawn-coloured robes girdled with a rich shawl, and a white turban, entered. He made his salute with grace and dignity to the Consul, touching his forehead, his lip, and his heart, and took his seat with the air of one not unaccustomed to be received, playing, until he received his chibouque, with a chaplet of beads.

"That is a good-looking fellow, Lothair," said St. Aldegonde; "or is it the dress that turns them out such swells? I feel quite a lout by some of these fellows."

"I think he would be good-looking in any dress," said Lothair. "A remarkable countenance."

It was an oval visage, with features in harmony with that form; large dark-brown eyes and lashes, and brows delicately but completely defined; no hair upon the face except a beard, full but not long. He seemed about the same age as Mr. Phœbus, and his complexion, though pale, was clear and fair.

The conversation after some rambling, had got upon the Suez Canal. Mr. Phœbus did not care for the political or the commercial consequences of that great enterprise, but he was glad that a natural division should be established between the greater races and the Ethiopian. It might not lead to any considerable result, but it asserted a principle. He looked upon that trench as a protest.

"But would you place the Nilotic family in the Ethiopian race?" enquired the Syrian in a voice commanding from its deep sweetness.

"I would certainly. They were Cushim, and that means negroes."

The Syrian did not agree with Mr. Phœbus; he stated his views firmly and clearly, but without urging them. He thought that we must look to the Pelasgi as the colonising race that had peopled and produced Egypt. The mention of the Pelasgi fired Mr. Phœbus to even unusual eloquence. He denounced the Pelasgi as a barbarous race: men of gloomy superstitions who, had it not been for the Hellenes, might have fatally arrested the human development. The triumph of the Hellenes was the triumph of the beautiful, and all that is great and good in life was owing to their victory.

"It is difficult to ascertain what is great in life," said the Syrian, "because nations differ on the subject and ages. Some, for example, consider war to be a great thing, others condemn it. I remember also when patriotism was a boast, and now it is a controversy. But it is not so difficult to ascertain what is good. For man has in his own being some guide to such knowledge, and divine aid to acquire it has not been wanting to him. For my part I could not maintain that the Hellenic system led to virtue."

The conversation was assuming an ardent character when the Consul, as a diplomatist, turned the
channel. Mr. Phœbus had vindicated the Hellenic
religion, the Syrian with a terse protest against the
religion of nature however idealised as tending to
the corruption of man, had let the question die
away, and the Divan were discussing dromedaries,
and dancing girls, and sherbet made of pomegranate
which the Consul recommended and ordered to be
produced. Some of the guests retired, and among
them the Syrian with the same salute and the same
graceful dignity as had distinguished his entrance.

"Who is that man?" said Mr. Phœbus. "I met
him at Rome ten years ago. Baron Mecklenburg
brought him to me to paint for my great picture of
St. John, which is in the gallery of Munich. He
said in his way—you remember his way—that he
would bring me a face of Paradise."

"I cannot exactly tell you his name," said the
Consul. "Prince Galitzin brought him here and
thought highly of him. I believe he is one of the
old Syrian families in the mountain; but whether he
be a Maronite, or a Druse, or anything else, I really
cannot say. Now try the sherbet."

CHAPTER XXXI.

THERE are few things finer than the morning view of Jerusalem from the Mount of Olives. The fresh and golden light falls on a walled city with turrets and towers and frequent gates: the houses of freestone with terraced or oval roofs sparkle in the sun while the cupolaed pile of the Church of the Holy Sepulchre, the vast monasteries, and the broad steep of Sion crowned with the Tower of David, vary the monotony of the general masses of building. But the glory of the scene is the Mosque of Omar as it rises on its broad platform of marble from the deep ravine of Kedron, with its magnificent dome high in the air, its arches and gardened courts, and its crescents glittering amid the cedar, the cypress, and the palm.

Reclining on Olivet, Lothair, alone and in charmed abstraction, gazed on the wondrous scene. Since his arrival at Jerusalem he lived much apart, nor had he found difficulty in effecting this isolation. Mr. Phœbus had already established a studio on a considerable scale, and was engaged in making sketches of pilgrims and monks, tall donkeys of Bethlehem with starry fronts, in which he much delighted, and grave Jellaheen sheiks who were hanging about the convents in the hopes of obtaining a convoy to the Dead Sea. As for St. Aldegonde and Bertram, they

passed their lives at the Russian Consulate, or with
its most charming inhabitants. This morning, with
the Consul and his wife and the matchless sisters,
as St. Aldegonde always termed them, they had gone
on an excursion to the Convent of the Nativity.
Dinner usually reassembled all the party, and then
the Divan followed.

"I say, Bertram," said St. Aldegonde, "what a
lucky thing we paired and went to Nubia! I rejoice
in the Divan, and yet somehow I cannot bear leaving those women. If the matchless sisters would
only smoke, by Jove they would be perfect!"

"I should not like Euphrosyne to smoke," said
Bertram.

A person approached Lothair by the pathway
from Bethany. It was the Syrian gentleman whom
he had met at the Consulate. As he was passing
Lothair, he saluted him with the grace which had
been before remarked, and Lothair, who was by
nature courteous, and even inclined a little to ceremony in his manners, especially with those with
whom he was not intimate, immediately rose, as he
would not receive such a salutation in a reclining
posture.

"Let me not disturb you," said the stranger,
"or if we must be on equal terms, let me also be
seated, for this is a view that never palls."

"It is perhaps familiar to you," said Lothair,
"but with me, only a pilgrim, its effect is fascinating,
almost overwhelming."

"The view of Jerusalem never becomes familiar,"
said the Syrian, "for its associations are so trans-

cendent, so various, so inexhaustible, that the mind
can never anticipate its course of thought and feeling, when one sits, as we do now, on this immortal
mount."

"I presume you live here?" said Lothair.

"Not exactly," said his companion. "I have
recently built a house without the walls, and I have
planted my hill with fruit trees and made vineyards
and olive grounds, but I have done this as much—
perhaps more—to set an example, which I am glad
to say has been followed, as for my own convenience
or pleasure. My home is in the North of Palestine
on the other side of Jordan, beyond the Sea of
Galilee. My family has dwelt there from time immemorial, but they always loved this city, and have
a legend that they dwelt occasionally within its walls,
even in the days when Titus from that hill looked
down upon the temple."

"I have often wished to visit the Sea of Galilee,"
said Lothair.

"Well, you have now an opportunity," said the
Syrian, "the North of Palestine, though it has no
tropical splendour, has much variety and a peculiar
natural charm. The burst and brightness of spring
have not yet quite vanished: you would find our
plains radiant with wild flowers, and our hills green
with young crops; and though we cannot rival Lebanon, we have forest glades among our famous
hills that when once seen are remembered."

"But there is something to me more interesting
than the splendour of tropical scenery," said Lo-

thair, "even if Galilee could offer it. I wish to visit the cradle of my faith."

"And you would do wisely," said the Syrian, "for there is no doubt the spiritual nature of man is developed in this land."

"And yet there are persons at the present day who doubt—even deny—the spiritual nature of man," said Lothair. "I do not, I could not—there are reasons why I could not."

"There are some things I know, and some things I believe," said the Syrian. "I know that I have a soul, and I believe that it is immortal."

"It is science that by demonstrating the insignificance of this globe in the vast scale of creation has led to this infidelity," said Lothair.

"Science may prove the insignificance of this globe in the scale of creation," said the stranger, "but it cannot prove the insignificance of man. What is the earth compared with the sun? a mole-hill by a mountain; yet the inhabitants of this earth can discover the elements of which the great orb consists and will probably ere long ascertain all the conditions of its being. Nay, the human mind can penetrate far beyond the sun. There is no relation therefore between the faculties of man and the scale in creation of the planet which he inhabits."

"I was glad to hear you assert the other night the spiritual nature of man in opposition to Mr. Phœbus."

"Ah! Mr. Phœbus!" said the stranger with a smile. "He is an old acquaintance of mine. And I must say he is very consistent—except in paying a visit to Jerusalem. That does surprise me. He said to me the other night the same things as he said to me at Rome many years ago. He would revive the worship of nature. The deities whom he so eloquently describes and so exquisitely delineates are the ideal personifications of the most eminent human qualities and chiefly the physical. Physical beauty is his standard of excellence, and he has a fanciful theory that moral order would be the consequence of the worship of physical beauty, for without moral order he holds physical beauty cannot be maintained. But the answer to Mr. Phœbus is, that his system has been tried and has failed, and under conditions more favourable than are likely to exist again; the worship of nature ended in the degradation of the human race."

"But Mr. Phœbus cannot really believe in Apollo and Venus," said Lothair. "These are phrases. He is, I suppose, what is called a Pantheist."

"No doubt the Olympus of Mr. Phœbus is the creation of his easel," replied the Syrian. "I should not, however, describe him as a Pantheist, whose creed requires more abstraction than Mr. Phœbus the worshipper of nature would tolerate. His school never care to pursue any investigation which cannot be followed by the eye—and the worship of the beautiful always ends in an orgy. As for Pantheism, it is Atheism in domino. The belief in a Creator who is unconscious of creating is more monstrous than any dogma of any of the Churches in this city, and we have them all here."

"But there are people now who tell you that

there never was any Creation, and therefore there never could have been a Creator," said Lothair.

"And which is now advanced with the confidence of novelty," said the Syrian, "though all of it has been urged and vainly urged thousands of years ago. There must be design, or all we see would be without sense, and I do not believe in the unmeaning. As for the natural forces to which all creation is now attributed, we know they are unconscious, while consciousness is as inevitable a portion of our existence as the eye or the hand. The conscious cannot be derived from the unconscious. Man is divine."

"I wish I could assure myself of the personality of the Creator," said Lothair. "I cling to that, but they say it is unphilosophical."

"In what sense?" asked the Syrian. "Is it more unphilosophical to believe in a personal God, omnipotent and omniscient, than in natural forces unconscious and irresistible? Is it unphilosophical to combine power with intelligence? Goethe, a Spinozist who did not believe in Spinoza, said that he could bring his mind to the conception that in the centre of space we might meet with a monad of pure intelligence. What may be the centre of space I leave to the dædal imagination of the author of 'Faust;' but a monad of pure intelligence—is that more philosophical than the truth, first revealed to man amid these everlasting hills," said the Syrian, "that God made man in His own image?"

"I have often found in that assurance a source of sublime consolation," said Lothair.

"It is the charter of the nobility of man," said the Syrian, "one of the divine dogmas revealed in this land; not the invention of Councils, not one of which was held on this sacred soil, confused assemblies first got together by the Greeks, and then by barbarous nations in barbarous times."

"Yet the divine land no longer tells us divine things," said Lothair.

"It may, or it may not, have fulfilled its destiny," said the Syrian. "'In My Father's house are many mansions,' and by the various families of nations the designs of the Creator are accomplished. God works by races, and one was appointed in due season and after many developments to reveal and expound in this land the spiritual nature of man. The Aryan and the Semite are of the same blood and origin, but when they quitted their central land they were ordained to follow opposite courses. Each division of the great race has developed one portion of the double nature of humanity, till after all their wanderings they met again, and, represented by their two choicest families, the Hellenes and the Hebrews, brought together the treasures of their accumulated wisdom and secured the civilisation of man."

"Those among whom I have lived of late," said Lothair, "have taught me to trust much in councils, and to believe that without them there could be no foundation for the Church. I observe you do not speak in that vein, though like myself you find solace in those dogmas which recognise the relations between the created and the Creator."

"There can be no religion without that recogni-

tion," said the Syrian, "and no creed can possibly
be devised without such a recognition that would
satisfy man.   Why we are here, whence we come,
whither we go—these are questions which man is
organically framed and forced to ask himself, and
that would not be the case if they could not be answered.   As for Churches depending on Councils,
the first Council was held more than three centuries
after the Sermon on the Mount.   We Syrians had
churches in the interval: no one can deny that.   I
bow before the Divine decree that swept them away
from Antioch to Jerusalem, but I am not yet prepared to transfer my spiritual allegiance to Italian
Popes and Greek Patriarchs.   We believe that our
family were among the first followers of Jesus, and
that we then held lands in Bashan which we hold
now.   We had a gospel once in our district where
there was some allusion to this, and being written
by neighbours, and probably at the time, I dare say
it was accurate, but the Western Churches declared
our gospel was not authentic, though why I cannot
tell, and they succeeded in extirpating it.   It was
not an additional reason why we should enter into
their fold.   So I am content to dwell in Galilee and
trace the footsteps of my divine Master; musing over
His life and pregnant sayings amid the mounts He
sanctified and the waters He loved so well."

The sun was now rising in the heavens, and the
hour had arrived when it became expedient to seek
the shade.   Lothair and the Syrian rose at the same
time.

"I shall not easily forget our conversation on

the Mount of Olives," said Lothair, "and I would
ask you to add to this kindness by permitting me,
before I leave Jerusalem, to pay my respects to you
under your roof."

"Peace be with you!" said the Syrian. "I live
without the gate of Damascus, on a hill which you
will easily recognise, and my name is PARACLETE."

CHAPTER XXXII.

TIME passed very agreeably to St. Aldegonde
and Bertram at Jerusalem, for it was passed entirely
at the Russian Consulate, or with its interesting and
charming inmates, who were always making excursions, or, as they styled them, pilgrimages. They
saw little of Lothair, who would willingly have conversed with his friend on many topics, but his friend
was almost always engaged, and if by some chance
they succeeded in finding themselves alone, Bertram
appeared to be always preoccupied. One day he
said to Lothair, "I tell you what, old fellow, if you
want to know all about what has happened at home,
I will give you Corisande's letters. They are a sort
of journal which she promised to keep for me, and
they will tell you everything. I found an immense
packet of them on our return from Cairo, and I
meant to have read them here; but I do not know
how it is—I suppose there is so much to be seen
here—but I never seem to have a moment to myself. I have got an engagement now to the Con-

sulate. We are going to Elisha's   untain to-day.
Why do not you come?"

"Well, I am engaged too," a: l Lothair. "I
have settled to go to the Tombs of t : Kings to-day,
with Signor Paraclete, and I cannot   ell get off; but
remember the letters."

The box of letters arrived at Lo air's rooms in
due season, and their perusal deeply interested him.
In their pages, alike earnest and livel , and a picture
of a mind of high intelligence ador ied with fancy
and feeling, the name of Lothair frequ ently appeared,
and sometimes accompanied with ε xpressions that
made his heart beat. All the rumour ı of his adventures as they gradually arrived in England, generally
distorted, were duly chronicled, and sometimes with
comments, which intimated the interest they occasioned to the correspondent of Bertram. More than
once she could not refrain from reproaching her
brother for having left his friend so much to himself.
"Of all your friends," she said, "the one who always most interested me, and seemed most worthy
of your affection." And then she deplored the absolute ruin of Lothair, for such she deemed his entrance into the Roman Church.

"I was right in my appreciation of that woman,
though I was utterly inexperienced in life," thought
Lothair. "If her mother had only favoured my
views two years ago, affairs would have been different. Would they have been better? Can they
be worse? But I have gained experience. Certainly;
and paid for it with my heart's blood. And might
I not have gained experience tranquilly, in the dis-

charge of the duties of my position at home—dear home? Perhaps not. And suppose I never had gained experience, I still might have been happy? And what am I now? Most lone and sad. So lone and sad, that nothing but the magical influence of the scene around me saves me from an overwhelming despondency."

Lothair passed his life chiefly with Paraclete, and a few weeks after their first acquaintance, they left Jerusalem together for Galilee.

The month of May had disappeared and June was advancing. Bertram and St. Aldegonde no longer talked about their pair, and their engagements in the House of Commons. There seemed a tacit understanding between them to avoid the subject; remarkable on the part of Bertram, for he had always been urgent on his brother-in-law to fulfil their parliamentary obligation.

The party at the Russian Consulate had gone on a grand expedition to the Dead Sea, and had been absent for many days from Jerusalem. They were convoyed by one of the sheiks of the Jordan valley. It was a most successful expedition—constant adventure, novel objects and habits, all the spell of a romantic life. The ladies were delighted with the scenery of the Jordan valley, and the gentlemen had good sport; St. Aldegonde had killed a wild boar, and Bertram an ibex, whose horns were preserved for Brentham. Mr. Phœbus intensely studied the camel and its habits. He persuaded himself that the ship of the desert entirely understood him. "But it is always so," he added. "There

is no animal that in a week does not perfectly comprehend me. Had I time and could give myself up
to it, I have no doubt I could make them speak.
Nature has endowed me, so far as dumb animals are
concerned, with a peculiar mesmeric power."

At last this happy caravan was again within sight
of the walls of Jerusalem.

"I should like to have remained in the valley of
the Jordan for ever," said St. Aldegonde.

"And so should I," whispered Bertram to Euphrosyne, "with the same companions."

When they had returned to the Consulate, they
found the post from England had arrived during
their absence. There were despatches for all. It is
an agitating moment—that arrival of letters in a distant land. Lord St. Aldegonde seemed much disturbed when he tore open and perused his. His
countenance became clouded; he dashed his hand
through his dishevelled locks; he pouted; and then
he said to Bertram, "Come to my room."

"Anything wrong at home?"

"Not at home," said St. Aldegonde. "Bertha is
all right. But a most infernal letter from Glyn—
most insolent. If I do return I will vote against
them. But I will not return. I have made up my
mind to that. People are so selfish," exclaimed St.
Aldegonde with indignation. "They never think of
anything but themselves."

"Show me his letter," said Bertram. "I have
got a letter too; it is from the Duke."

The letter of the Opposition whip did not deserve the epithets ascribed to it by St. Aldegonde.

It was urgent and courteously peremptory; but, considering the circumstances of the case, by no means too absolute. Paired to Easter by great indulgence, St. Aldegonde was passing Whitsuntide at Jerusalem. The parliamentary position was critical, and the future of the Opposition seemed to depend on the majority by which their resolutions on the Irish Church were sent up to the House of Lords.

"Well," said Bertram. "I see nothing to complain of in that letter. Except a little more urgency, it is almost the same language as reached us at Cairo, and then you said Glyn was a capital fellow, and seemed quite pleased."

"Yes, because I hated Egypt," said St. Aldegonde. "I hated the Pyramids, and I was disappointed with the dancing-girls; and it seemed to me that, if it had not been for the whip, we never should have been able to escape. But things are very different now."

"Yes they are," said Bertram in a melancholy tone.

"You do not think of returning?" said St. Aldegonde.

"Instantly," replied Bertram. "I have a letter from the Duke which is peremptory. The county is dissatisfied with my absence. And mine is a queer constituency; very numerous and several large towns; the popularity of my family gained me the seat, not their absolute influence."

"My constituents never trouble me," said St. Aldegonde.

"You have none," said Bertram.

"Well, if I were member for a metropolitan district I would not budge. And I little thought you would have deserted me."

"Ah!" sighed Bertram. "You are discontented, because your amusements are interrupted. But think of my position, torn from a woman whom I adore."

"Well, you know you must have left her sooner or later," urged St. Aldegonde.

"Why?" asked Bertram.

"You know what Lothair told us. She is engaged to her cousin the Prince of Samos, and——"

"If I had only the Prince of Samos to deal with I should care little," said Bertram.

"Why, what do you mean?"

"That Euphrosyne is mine, if my family will sanction our union, but not otherwise."

St. Aldegonde gave a long whistle, and he added, "I wish Bertha were here. She is the only person I know who has a head."

"You see, my dear Granville, while you are talking of your little disappointments, I am involved in awful difficulties."

"You are sure about the Prince of Samos?"

"Clear your head of that. There is no engagement of any kind between him and Euphrosyne. The visit to the island was only a preliminary ceremony—just to show himself. No doubt the father wishes the alliance; nor is there any reason to suppose that it would be disagreeable to the son; but, I repeat it—no engagement exists."

"If I were not your brother-in-law, I should have

been very glad to have married Euphrosyne myself,"
said St. Aldegonde.

"Yes, but what am I to do?" asked Bertram
rather impatiently.

"It will not do to write to Brentham," said St.
Aldegonde, gravely; "that I see clearly." Then,
after musing a while, he added, "I am vexed to
leave our friends here and shall miss them sadly.
They are the most agreeable people I ever knew. I
never enjoyed myself so much. But we must think
of nothing but your affairs. We must return instantly.
The whip will be an excuse, but the real business
will be Euphrosyne. I should delight in having her
for a sister-in-law, but the affair will require management. We can make short work of getting home:
steam to Marseilles, leave the yacht there, and take
the railroad. I have half a mind to telegraph to
Bertha to meet us there. She would be of great
use."

CHAPTER XXXIII.

LOTHAIR was delighted with Galilee, and particularly with the blue waters of its lake slumbering beneath the surrounding hills. Of all its once pleasant towns, Tiberias alone remains, and that in ruins from a recent earthquake. But where are Chorazin, and Bethsaida, and Capernaum? A group of hovels and an ancient tower still bear the magic name of Magdala, and all around are green mounts and gentle slopes, the scenes of miracles that softened the heart of man, and of sermons that never tire his ear. Dreams passed over Lothair of settling for ever on the shores of these waters and of reproducing all their vanished happiness: rebuilding their memorable cities, reviving their fisheries, cultivating the plain of Gennesaret and the country of the Gadarenes, and making researches in this cradle of pure and primitive Christianity.

The heritage of Paraclete was among the oaks of Bashan, a lofty land, rising suddenly from the Jordan valley, verdant and well watered, and clothed in many parts with forest; there the host of Lothair resided among his lands and people, and himself dwelt in a stone and castellated building, a portion of which was of immemorial antiquity, and where he could rally his forces and defend himself in case of the irruption and invasion of the desert tribes. And

here one morn arrived a messenger from Jerusalem
summoning Lothair back to that city, in consequence
of the intended departure of his friends.

The call was urgent and was obeyed immediately
with that promptitude, which the manners of the
East, requiring no preparation, admit.   Paraclete
accompanied his guest.   They had to cross the Jordan, and then to trace their way till they reached
the southern limit of the plain of Esdraelon, from
whence they counted on the following day to reach
Jerusalem. While they were encamped on this spot,
a body of Turkish soldiery seized all their horses,
which were required, they said, by the Pacha of
Damascus, who was proceeding to Jerusalem attending a great Turkish general, who was on a mission
to examine the means of defence of Palestine on the
Egyptian side.   This was very vexatious, but one of
those incidents of Eastern life against which it is
impossible to contend; so Lothair and Paraclete were
obliged to take refuge in their pipes beneath a huge
and solitary sycamore tree, awaiting the arrival of
the Ottoman magnificoes.

They came at last, a considerable force of cavalry,
then mules and barbarous carriages with the harem,
all the riders and inmates enveloped in what appeared to be winding sheets, white and shapeless;
about them eunuchs and servants.   The staff of the
Pachas followed, preceding the grandees who closed
the march, mounted on Anatolian chargers.

Paraclete and Lothair had been obliged to leave
the grateful shade of the sycamore tree as the spot
had been fixed on by the commander of the ad-

vanced guard for the resting-place of the Pachas. They were standing aside and watching the progress of the procession, and contemplating the earliest opportunity of representing their grievances to high authority, when the Turkish general, or the Seraskier, as the Syrians inaccurately styled him, suddenly reined in his steed, and said in a loud voice, "Captain Muriel."

Lothair recognised the well-known voice of his commanding officer in the Apennine, and advanced to him with a military salute. "I must first congratulate you on being alive, which I hardly hoped," said the General. "Then let me know why you are here."

And Lothair told him.

"Well, you shall have back your horses," said the General; "and I will escort you to El Khuds. In the meantime you must be our guest;" and he presented him to the Pacha of Damascus with some form. "You and I have bivouacked in the open air before this, and not in so bland a clime."

Beneath the shade of the patriarchal sycamore, the General narrated to Lothair his adventures since they were fellow-combatants on the fatal field of Mentana.

"When all was over," continued the General, "I fled with Garibaldi, and gained the Italian frontier at Terni. Here we were of course arrested by the authorities; but not very maliciously. I escaped one morning, and got among the mountains in the neighbourhood of our old camp. I had to wander about these parts for some time, for the Papalini were in the vicinity, and there was danger. It was a hard time; but I found a friend now and then among the country people, though they are dreadfully superstitious. At last I got to the shore, and induced an honest fellow to put to sea in an open boat on the chance of something turning up. It did in the shape of a brigantine from Elba bound for Corfou. Here I was sure to find friends, for the brotherhood are strong in the Ionian Isles. And I began to look about for business. The Greeks made me some offers, but their schemes were all vanity, worse than the Irish. You remember our Fenian squabble? From something that transpired, I had made up my mind, so soon as I was well equipped, to go to Turkey. I had had some transactions with the house of Cantacuzene, through the kindness of our dear friend whom we will never forget, but will never mention; and through them I became acquainted with the Prince of Samos, who is the chief of their house. He is in the entire confidence of Aali Pacha. I soon found out that there was real business on the carpet. The Ottoman army, after many trials and vicissitudes, is now in good case; and the Porte has resolved to stand no more nonsense either in this direction" and the General gave a significant glance, "or in any other. But they wanted a general; they wanted a man who knew his business. I am not a Garibaldi, you know, and never pretended to be. I have no genius, or volcanic fire, or that sort of thing; but I do presume to say, with fair troops, paid with tolerable regularity, a battery or two of rifled cannon, and a well-organised commissariat, I am not afraid of meeting

any captain of my acquaintance, whatever his land
or language. The Turks are a brave people, and
there is nothing in their system, political or religious,
which jars with my convictions. In the army, which
is all that I much care for, there is the career of
merit, and I can promote any able man that I recognise. As for their religion, they are tolerant and
exact nothing from me; and if I had any religion
except Madre Natura, I am not sure I would not
prefer Islamism; which is at least simple, and as
little sacerdotal as any organised creed can be. The
Porte made me a liberal offer and I accepted it. It
so happened that, the moment I entered their service,
I was wanted. They had a difficulty on their Dal-
matian frontier; I settled it in a way they liked.
And now I am sent here with full powers, and am
a pacha of the highest class, and with a prospect of
some warm work. I do not know what your views
are, but, if you would like a little more soldiering,
I will put you on my staff; and, for ought I know,
we may find our winter-quarters at Grand Cairo—
they say a pleasant place for such a season."

"My soldiering has not been very fortunate,"
said Lothair; "and I am not quite as great an admirer of the Turks as you are, General. My mind
is rather on the pursuits of peace, and twenty hours
ago I had a dream of settling on the shores of the
sea of Galilee."

"Whatever you do," said the General, "give up
dreams."

"I think you may be right in that," said Lothair,
with half a sigh.

"Action may not always be happiness," said the General; "but there is no happiness without action. If you will not fight the Egyptians, were I you, I would return home and plunge into affairs. That was a fine castle of yours I visited one morning; a man who lives in such a place must be able to find a great deal to do."

"I almost wish I were there, with you for my companion," said Lothair.

"The wheel may turn," said the General; "but I begin to think I shall not see much of Europe again. I have given it some of my best years and best blood; and if I had assisted in establishing the Roman republic, I should not have lived in vain; but the old imposture seems to me stronger than ever. I have got ten good years in me yet; and, if I be well supported and in luck, for, after all, everything depends on fortune, and manage to put a couple of hundred thousand men in perfect discipline, I may find some consolation for not blowing up St. Peter's, and may do something for the freedom of mankind on the banks of the Danube."

CHAPTER XXXIV.

MRS. PUTNEY GILES in full toilette was standing before the mantel-piece of her drawing-room in Hyde Park Gardens, and watching with some anxiety the clock that rested on it. It was the dinner hour, and Mr. Putney Giles, particular in such matters, had not returned. No one looked forward to his dinner and a chat with his wife with greater zest than Mr. Putney Giles; and he deserved the gratification which both incidents afforded him, for he fairly earned it. Full of news and bustle, brimful of importance and prosperity, sunshiny and successful, his daily return home—which, with many, perhaps most, men is a process lugubriously monotonous—was in Hyde Park Gardens, even to Apollonia, who possessed many means of amusement and occupation, a source ever of interest and excitement.

To-day too, particularly, for their great client, friend, and patron, Lothair, had arrived last night from the Continent at Muriel House, and had directed Mr. Putney Giles to be in attendance on him on the afternoon of this day.

Muriel House was a family mansion in the Green Park. It was built of hewn stone during the last century—a Palladian edifice, for a time much neglected, but now restored and duly prepared for the reception of its lord and master by the same com-

bined energy and taste which had proved so satisfactory and successful at Muriel Towers.

It was a long room, the front saloon at Hyde
Park Gardens, and the door was as remote as possible from the mantel-piece. It opened suddenly,
but only the panting face of Mr. Putney Giles was
seen, as he poured forth in hurried words: "My
dear, dreadfully late, but I can dress in five minutes.
I only opened the door in passing, to tell you that
I have seen our great friend; wonderful man! but
I will tell you all at dinner, or after. It was not he
who kept me, but the Duke of Brecon. The Duke
has been with me two hours. I had a good mind
to bring him home to dinner, and give him a bottle
of my '48. They like that sort of thing; but it will
keep," and the head vanished.

The Duke of Brecon would not have dined ill
had he honoured this household. It is a pleasant
thing to see an opulent and prosperous man of
business, sanguine and full of health, and a little
overworked, at that royal meal, dinner. How he
enjoys his soup! And how curious in his fish! How
critical in his entrée, and how nice in his Welsh
mutton! His exhausted brain rallies under the glass
of dry sherry, and he realises all his dreams with
the aid of claret that has the true flavour of the
violet.

"And now, my dear Apollonia," said Mr. Putney Giles, when the servants had retired, and he
turned his chair and played with a new nut from
the Brazils, "about our great friend. Well, I was
there at two o'clock, and found him at breakfast. In-

deed, he said, that had he not given me an appoint-
ment, he thought he should not have risen at all.
So delighted he was to find himself again in an
English bed. Well, he told me everything that had
happened. I never knew a man so unreserved, and
so different from what he was when I first knew
him, for he never much cared then to talk about
himself. But no egotism, nothing of that sort of
thing—all his mistakes, all his blunders, as he called
them. He told me everything that I might thoroughly
understand his position, and that he might judge
whether the steps I had taken in reference to it were
adequate."

"I suppose about his religion," said Apollonia.
"What is he after all?"

"As sound as you are. But you are right; that
was the point on which he was most anxious. He
wrote, you know, to me from Malta, when the account of his conversion first appeared, to take all
necessary steps to contradict the announcement, and
counteract its consequences. He gave me carte
blanche, and was anxious to know precisely what I
had done. I told him that a mere contradiction,
anonymous or from a third person, however unquali-
fied its language, would have no effect in the face
of a detailed narrative, like that in all the papers, of
his walking in procession and holding a lighted
taper and all that sort of thing. What I did was
this. I commenced building, by his direction, two
new churches on his estate, and announced in the
local journals, copied in London, that he would be
present at the consecration of both. I subscribed in

his name, and largely, to all the diocesan societies, gave a thousand pounds to the Bishop of London's fund, and accepted for him the office of steward for this year for the Sons of the Clergy. Then, when the public feeling was ripe, relieved from all its anxieties, and beginning to get indignant at the calumnies that had been so freely circulated, the time for paragraphs had arrived, and one appeared stating that a discovery had taken place of the means by which an unfounded and preposterous account of the conversion of a distinguished young English nobleman at Rome had been invented and circulated, and would probably furnish the occasion for an action for libel. And now his return and appearance at the Chapel Royal next Sunday will clench the whole business."

"And he was satisfied?"

"Most satisfied; a little anxious whether his personal friends, and particularly the Brentham family, were assured of the truth. He travelled home with the Duke's son and Lord St. Aldegonde, but they came from remote parts, and their news from home was not very recent."

"And how does he look?"

"Very well; never saw him look better. He is handsomer than he was. But he is changed. I could not conceive in a year that any one could be so changed. He was young for his years; he is now old for his years. He was, in fact, a boy; he is now a man; and yet it is only a year. He said it seemed to him ten."

"He has been through a fiery furnace," said
Apollonia.

"Well, he has borne it well," said Mr. Giles.
"It is worth while serving such a client, so cordial,
so frank, and yet so full of thought. He says he
does not in the least regret all the money he has
wasted. Had he remained at home, it would have
gone to building a cathedral."

"And a Popish one!" said Apollonia. "I cannot
agree with him," she continued, "that his Italian
campaign was a waste of money. It will bear fruit.
We shall still see the end of the 'abomination of
desolation.'"

"Very likely," said Mr. Giles; "but I trust my
client will have no more to do with such questions
either way."

"And did he ask after his friends?" said Apollonia.

"Very much: he asked after you. I think he
went through all the guests at Muriel Towers except
the poor Campians. He spoke to me about the
Colonel, to whom it appears he has written; but
Theodora he never mentioned, except by some peri-
phrasis, some allusion to a great sorrow, or to some
dear friend whom he had lost. He seems a little
embarrassed about the St. Jeromes, and said more
than once that he owed his life to Miss Arundel.
He dwelt a good deal upon this. He asked also a
great deal about the Brentham family. They seem
the people whom he most affects. When I told him
of Lady Corisande's approaching union with the
Duke of Brecon, I did not think he half liked it."

"But is it settled?"

"The same as. The Duke has been with me two hours to-day about his arrangements. He has proposed to the parents, who are delighted with the match, and has received every encouragement from the young lady. He looks upon it as certain."

"I wish our kind friend had not gone abroad," said Apollonia.

"Well, at any rate, he has come back," said Mr. Giles; "that is something. I am sure I more than once never expected to see him again."

"He has every virtue, and every charm," said Apollonia, "and principles that are now proved. I shall never forget his kindness at the Towers. I wish he were settled for life. But who is worthy of him? I hope he will not fall into the clutches of that Popish girl. I have sometimes, from what I observed at Muriel and other reasons, a dread misgiving."

CHAPTER XXXV.

IT was the first night that Lothair had slept in his own house, and, when he awoke in the morning, he was quite bewildered, and thought for a moment he was in the Palazzo Agostini. He had not reposed in so spacious and lofty a chamber since he was at Rome. And this brought all his recollection to his Roman life, and everything that had happened there, "and yet, after all," he said, "had it not been for Clare Arundel, I should never have seen Muriel House. I owe to her my life." His relations with the St. Jerome family were doubtless embarrassing, even painful; and yet his tender and susceptible nature could not for a moment tolerate that he should passively submit to an estrangement from those who had conferred on him so much kindness, and whose ill-considered and injurious courses, as he now esteemed them, were perhaps, and probably, influenced and inspired by exalted, even sacred, motives.

He wondered whether they were in London; and if so, what should he do? Should he call, or should he write? He wished he could do something to show to Miss Arundel how much he appreciated her kindness, and how grateful he was. She was a fine creature, and all her errors were noble ones; enthusiasm, energy, devotion to a sublime cause.

Errors, but are these errors? Are they not, on the contrary, qualities which should command admiration in anyone?—and in a woman and a beautiful woman, more than admiration?

There is always something to worry you. It comes as regularly as sunrise. Here was Lothair under his own roof again, after strange and trying vicissitudes, with his health restored, his youth little diminished, with some strange memories and many sweet ones; on the whole, once more in great prosperity, and yet his mind harped only on one vexing thought, and that was his painful and perplexed relations with the St. Jerome family.

His thoughts were a little distracted from this harassing theme by the novelty of his house and the pleasure it gave him. He admired the double staircase and the somewhat heavy, yet richly carved ceilings; and the look into the park, shadowy and green, with a rich summer sun and the palace in the distance. What an agreeable contrast to his hard noisy sojourn in a bran-new, brobdignagian hotel, as was his coarse fate when he was launched into London life. This made him think of many comforts for which he ought to be grateful, and then he remembered Muriel Towers and how completely and capitally everything was there prepared and appointed, and while he was thinking over all this and kindly of the chief author of these satisfactory arrangements, and the instances in which that individual had shown, not merely professional dexterity and devotion, but some of the higher qualities that make life sweet and pleasant, Mr. Putney Giles was announced, and Lothair sprang forward and gave him his hand with a cordiality which repaid at once that perfect, but large-hearted, lawyer for all his exertions, and some anxieties that he had never expressed even to Apollonia.

Nothing in life is more remarkable than the unnecessary anxiety which we endure, and generally occasion ourselves. Between four and five o'clock, having concluded his long conference with Mr. Putney Giles, Lothair, as if he were traversing the principal street of a foreign town, or rather treading on tiptoe like a prince in some enchanted castle, ventured to walk down St. James's Street, and the very first person he met was Lord St. Jerome!

Nothing could be more unaffectedly hearty, than his greeting by that good man and thorough gentleman. "I saw by the 'Post,' you had arrived," said Lord St. Jerome, "and we were all saying at breakfast how glad we should be to see you again. And looking so well. Quite yourself! I never saw you looking better. You have been to Egypt with Lord St. Aldegonde, I think? It was the wisest thing you could do. I said to Gertrude when you went to Sicily, 'If I were Lothair, I would go a good deal farther than Sicily.' You wanted change of scene and air, more than any man I know."

"And how are they all?" said Lothair; "my first visit will be to them."

"And they will be delighted to see you. Lady St. Jerome is a little indisposed; a cold caught at one of her bazaars. She will hold them, and they say that no one ever sells so much. But still, as I often say, my dear Gertrude, would it not be better if I were to give you a cheque for the institution; it would be the same to them, and would save you a great deal of trouble. But she fancies her presence inspires others, and perhaps there is something in it."

"I doubt not; and Miss Arundel?"

"Clare is quite well, and I am hurrying home now to ride with her. I shall tell her that you asked after her."

"And offer her my kindest remembrances."

"What a relief!" exclaimed Lothair when once more alone. "I thought I should have sunk into the earth when he first addressed me, and now I would not have missed this meeting for any consideration."

He had not the courage to go into White's. He was under a vague impression that the whole population of the metropolis, and especially those who reside in the sacred land, bounded on the one side by Piccadilly and on the other by Pall Mall, were unceasingly talking of his scrapes and misadventures; but he met Lord Carisbrooke and Mr. Brancepeth.

"Ah! Lothair," said Carisbrooke; "I do not think we have seen you this season; certainly not since Easter. What have you been doing with yourself?"

"You have been in Egypt?" said Mr. Brancepeth. "The Duke was mentioning at White's to-day that you had returned with his son and Lord St. Aldegonde."

"And does it pay?" enquired Carisbrooke. "Egypt? What I have found generally in this sort of thing is, that one hardly knows what to do with one's evenings."

"There is something in that," said Lothair, "and perhaps it applies to other countries besides Egypt. However, though it is true I did return with St. Aldegonde and Bertram, I have myself not been to Egypt."

"And where did you pick them up?"

"At Jerusalem."

"Jerusalem! What on earth could they go to Jerusalem for?" said Lord Carisbrooke. "I am told there is no sort of sport there. They say, in the Upper Nile, there is good shooting."

"St. Aldegonde was disappointed. I suppose our countrymen have disturbed the crocodiles and frightened away the pelicans?"

"We were going to look in at White's—come with us."

Lothair was greeted with general kindness; but nobody seemed aware that he had been long and unusually absent from them. Some had themselves not come up to town till after Easter, and had therefore less cause to miss him. The great majority, however, were so engrossed with themselves that they never missed anybody. The Duke of Brecon appealed to Lothair about something that had happened at the last Derby, and was under the impression, until better informed, that Lothair had been one of his party. There were some exceptions to . this general unacquaintance with events which an hour before Lothair had feared fearfully engrossed society. Hugo Bohun was doubly charmed to see him, "because we were all in a fright one day that they were going to make you a cardinal, and it turned out that, at the very time they said you were about to enter the conclave, you happened to be at the second cataract. What lies these newspapers do tell!"

But the climax of relief was reached when the noble and grey-headed patron of the arts in Great Britain approached him with polished benignity, and said, "I can give you perhaps even later news than you can give me of our friends at Jerusalem. I had a letter from Madame Phœbus this morning, and she mentioned with great regret that you had just left them. Your first travels, I believe?"

"My first."

"And wisely planned. You were right in starting out and seeing the distant parts. One may not always have the energy which such an expedition requires. You can keep Italy for a later and calmer day."

Thus, one by one, all the cerulean demons of the morn had vanished, and Lothair had nothing to worry him. He felt a little dull as the dinner hour approached. Bertram was to dine at home, and then go to the House of Commons; St. Aldegonde concluding the day with the same catastrophe, had in the most immoral manner, in the interval, gone to the play to see "School," of which he had read an account in Galignani when he was in quarantine.

Lothair was so displeased with this unfeeling conduct on his part that he declined to accompany him; but Lady St. Aldegonde, who dined at Crecy House, defended her husband, and thought it very right and reasonable that one so fond of the drama as he, who had been so long deprived of gratifying his taste in that respect, should take the first opportunity of enjoying this innocent amusement. A solitary dinner at Muriel House, in one of those spacious and lofty chambers, rather appalled Lothair, and he was getting low again, remembering nothing but his sorrows, when Mr. Pinto came up to him and said, "The impromptu is always successful in life; you cannot be engaged to dinner, for everybody believes you are at Jericho. What say you to dining with me? Less than the Muses and more than the Graces, certainly, if you come. Lady Beatrice has invited herself, and she is to pick up a lady, and I was to look out for a couple of agreeable men. Hugo is coming, and you will complete the charm."

"The spell then is complete," said Lothair, "I suppose a late eight."

CHAPTER XXXVL

LOTHAIR was breakfasting alone on the morrow, when his servant announced the arrival of Mr. Ruby, who had been ordered to be in attendance.

"Show him up," said Lothair, "and bring me the despatch-box which is in my dressing-room."

Mr. Ruby was deeply gratified to be again in the presence of a nobleman so eminently distinguished, both for his property and his taste, as Lothair. He was profuse in his congratulations to his Lordship on his return to his native land, while at the same time he was opening a bag, from which he extracted a variety of beautiful objects, none of them for sale, all executed commissions, which were destined to adorn the fortunate and the fair. "This is lovely, my lord, quite new, for the Queen of Madagascar; for the Empress this, Her Majesty's own design, at least almost. Lady Melton's bridal necklace, and my Lord's George, the last given by King James II.; broken up during the Revolution, but reset by us from an old drawing with picked stones."

"Very pretty," said Lothair; "but it is not exactly this sort of thing that I want. See," and he opened the despatch-box, and took from out of it a crucifix. It was made of some Eastern wood, inlaid with mother-of-pearl; the figure carved in brass, though not without power, and at the end of each of the

four terminations of the cross was a small cavity
enclosing something, and covered with glass.

"See," continued Lothair, "this is the crucifix,
given with a carved shell to each pilgrim who visits
the Holy Sepulchre. Within these four cavities is
earth from the four holy places: Calvary, Sion, Bethlehem, and Gethsemane. Now what I want is a
crucifix, something of this dimension, but made of
the most costly materials; the figure must be of pure
gold; I should like the cross to be of choice emeralds,
which I am told are now more precious even than
brilliants, and I wish the earth of the sacred places
to be removed from this crucifix, and introduced in
a similar manner into the one which you are to
make; and each cavity must be covered with a slit
diamond. Do you understand?"

"I follow you, my Lord," said Mr. Ruby, with
glistening eyes. "It will be a rare jewel. Is there
to be a limit as to the cost?"

"None but such as taste and propriety suggest,"
said Lothair. "You will of course make a drawing
and an estimate, and send them to me; but I desire
despatch."

When Mr. Ruby had retired, Lothair took from
the despatch-box a sealed packet, and looked at it
for some moments, and then pressed it to his lips.

In the afternoon, Lothair found himself again in
the saddle, and was riding about London, as if he
had never quitted it. He left his cards at Crecy
House, and many other houses, and he called at the
St. Jeromes late, but asked if they were at home.
He had reckoned that they would not be, and his

reckoning was right. It was impossible to conceal from himself that it was a relief. Mr. Putney Giles dined alone with Lothair this evening, and they talked over many things; among others the approaching marriage of Lady Corisande with the Duke of Brecon.

"Everybody marries except myself," said Lothair rather peevishly.

"But your Lordship is too young to think of that yet," said Mr. Putney Giles.

"I feel very old," said Lothair.

At this moment there arrived a note from Bertram, saying his mother was quite surprised and disappointed that Lothair had not asked to see her in the morning. She had expected him as a matter of course at luncheon, and begged that he would come on the morrow.

"I have had many pleasant luncheons in that house," said Lothair, "but this will be the last. When all the daughters are married nobody eats luncheon."

"That would hardly apply to this family," said Mr. Putney Giles, who always affected to know everything, and generally did. "They are so united, that I fancy the famous luncheons at Crecy House will always go on, and be a popular mode of their all meeting."

"I half agree with St. Aldegonde," said Lothair grumbling to himself, "that if one is to meet that Duke of Brecon every day at luncheon, for my part I had rather stay away."

In the course of the evening there also arrived

invitations to all the impending balls and assemblies
for Lothair, and there seemed little prospect of his
again being forced to dine with his faithful solicitor
as a refuge from melancholy.

On the morrow he went in his brougham to
Crecy House, and he had such a palpitation of the
heart when he arrived, that for a moment he absolutely thought he must retire. His mind was full of
Jerusalem, the Mount of Olives, and the Sea of
Galilee. He was never nervous there, never agitated,
never harassed, no palpitations of the heart, no dread
suspense. There was repose alike of body and soul.
Why did he ever leave Palestine and Paraclete? He
should have remained in Syria for ever, cherishing
in a hallowed scene a hallowed sorrow, of which
even the bitterness was exalted and ennobling.

He stood for a moment in the great hall at Crecy
House, and the groom of the chambers in vain
solicited his attention. It was astonishing how much
passed through his mind while the great clock hardly
described sixty seconds. But in that space he had
reviewed his life, arrived at the conclusion that all
was vanity and bitterness, that he had failed in
everything, was misplaced, had no object and no
hope, and that a distant and unbroken solitude in
some scene where either the majesty of nature was
overwhelming or its moral associations were equally
sublime, must be his only refuge. In the meditation
of the Cosmos, or in the divine reverie of sacred
lands, the burthen of existence might be endured.

"Her Grace is at luncheon, my Lord," at length
said the groom of the chambers, and Lothair was

ushered into the gay and festive and cordial scene.
The number of the self-invited guests alone saved
him. His confusion was absolute, and the Duchess
remarked afterwards that Lothair seemed to have
regained all his shyness.

When Lothair had rallied and could survey the
scene, he found he was sitting by his hostess; that
the Duke, not a luncheon man, was present, and, as
it turned out afterwards, for the pleasure of meeting
Lothair. Bertram also was present, and several
married daughters, and Lord Montairy, and Captain
Mildmay, and one or two others; and next to Lady
Corisande was the Duke of Brecon.

So far as Lothair was concerned, the luncheon
was unsuccessful. His conversational powers deserted
him. He answered in monosyllables, and never
originated a remark. He was greatly relieved when
they rose and returned to the gallery in which they
seemed all disposed to linger. The Duke approached
him, and in his mood he found it easier to talk to
men than to women. Male conversation is of a
coarser grain, and does not require so much play of
thought and manner: discourse about Suez Canal,
and Arab horses, and pipes and pachas, can be carried on without any psychological effort, and by
degrees banishes all sensibility. And yet he was
rather dreamy, talked better than he listened, did
not look his companion in the face as the Duke
spoke, which was his custom, and his eye was wandering. Suddenly, Bertram having joined them and
speaking to his father, Lothair darted away and ap-

proached Lady Corisande, whom Lady Montairy had
just quitted.

"As I may never have the opportunity again,"
said Lothair, "let me thank you, Lady Corisande,
for some kind thoughts which you deigned to bestow
on me in my absence."

His look was serious; his tone almost sad.
Neither were in keeping with the scene and the
apparent occasion; and Lady Corisande, not displeased, but troubled, murmured—"Since I last met
you, I heard you had seen much and suffered
much."

"And that makes the kind thoughts of friends
more precious," said Lothair. "I have few: your
brother is the chief, but even he never did me any
kindness so great as when he told me that you had
spoken of me with sympathy."

"Bertram's friends are mine," said Lady Corisande, "but, otherwise, it would be impossible for
us all not to feel an interest in——, one of whom
we had seen so much," she added with some hesitation.

"Ah! Brentham!" said Lothair, "dear Brentham!
Do you remember once saying to me that you hoped
you should never leave Brentham?"

"Did I say so?" said Lady Corisande.

"I wish I had never left Brentham," said Lothair;
"it was the happiest time of my life. I had not
then a sorrow or a care."

"But everybody has sorrows and cares," said
Lady Corisande; "you have, however, a great many
things which ought to make you happy."

"I do not deserve to be happy," said Lothair, "for I have made so many mistakes. My only consolation is that one great error which you most deprecated I have escaped."

"Take a brighter and a nobler view of your life," said Lady Corisande; "feel rather you have been tried and not found wanting."

At this moment the Duchess approached them and interrupted their conversation; and soon after this Lothair left Crecy House, still moody but less despondent.

There was a ball at Lady Clanmorne's in the evening, and Lothair was present. He was astonished at the number of new faces he saw, the new phrases he heard, the new fashions alike in dress and manner. He could not believe it was the same world that he had quitted only a year ago. He was glad to take refuge with Hugo Bohun as with an old friend, and could not refrain from expressing to that eminent person his surprise at the novelty of all around him.

"It is you, my dear Lothair," replied Hugo, "that is surprising,—not the world—that has only developed in your absence. What could have induced a man like you to be away for a whole season from the scene! Our forefathers might afford to travel—the world was then stereotyped. It will not do to be out of sight now. It is very well for St. Aldegonde to do these things, for the great object of St. Aldegonde is not to be in society, and he has never succeeded in his object. But here is the new beauty."

16*

There was a stir and a sensation. Men made
way and even women retreated—and, leaning on
the arm of Lord Carisbrooke, in an exquisite costume
that happily displayed her splendid figure, and
radiant with many charms, swept by a lady of commanding mien and stature, self-possessed and even
grave, when suddenly turning her head, her pretty
face broke into enchanting dimples as she exclaimed,
"O! cousin Lothair!"

Yes, the beautiful giantesses of Muriel Towers
had become the beauties of the season. Their success had been as sudden and immediate as it was
complete and sustained.

"Well, this is stranger than all!" said Lothair
to Hugo Bohun when Lady Flora had passed on.

"The only persons talked of," said Hugo. "I
am proud of my previous acquaintance with them. I
think Carisbrooke has serious thoughts; but there are
some who prefer Lady Grizell."

"Lady Corisande was your idol last season," said
Lothair.

"Oh! she is out of the running," said Hugo;
"she is finished. But I have not heard yet of any
day being fixed. I wonder when he marries whether
Brecon will keep on his theatre."

"His theatre!".

"Yes; the high mode now for a real swell is to
have a theatre. Brecon has the Frolic; Kate Simmons is his manager, who calls herself Athalie de
Montfort. You ought to have a theatre, Lothair;
and if there is not one to hire, you should build
one. It would show that you were alive again and

had the spirit of an English noble, and atone for some of your eccentricities."

"But I have no Kate Simmons who calls herself Athalie de Montfort," said Lothair; "I am not so favoured, Hugo. However, I might succeed Brecon, as I hardly suppose he will maintain such an establishment when he is married."

"I beg your pardon," rejoined Hugo. "It is the thing. Several of our greatest swells have theatres and are married. In fact, a first-rate man should have everything, and therefore he ought to have both a theatre and a wife."

"Well, I do not think your manners have improved since last year, or your morals," said Lothair. "I have half a mind to go down to Muriel, and shut myself up there."

He walked away and sauntered into the ballroom. The first forms he recognised were Lady Corisande waltzing with the Duke of Brecon, who was renowned for this accomplishment. The heart of Lothair felt bitter. He remembered his stroll to the dairy with the Duchess at Brentham, and their conversation. Had his views then been acceded to how different would have been his lot! And it was not his fault that they had been rejected. And yet, had they been accomplished, would they have been happy? The character of Corisande, according to her mother, was not then formed, nor easily scrutable. Was it formed now? and what were its bent and genius? And his own character? It could not be denied that his mind was somewhat crude then, and his general conclusions on life and duty hardly suf-

ficiently matured and developed to offer a basis for
domestic happiness on which one might confidently
depend.

And Theodora? Had he married then he should
never have known Theodora. In this bright saloon,
amid the gaiety of festive music, and surrounded by
gliding forms of elegance and brilliancy, his heart
was full of anguish when he thought of Theodora.
To have known such a woman and to have lost her!
Why should a man live after this? Yes; he would
retire to Muriel, once hallowed by her presence, and
he would raise to her memory some monumental
fane, beyond the dreams even of Artemisia, and
which should commemorate alike her wondrous life
and wondrous mind.

A beautiful hand was extended to him, and a
fair face, animated with intelligence, welcomed him
without a word. It was Lady St. Jerome. Lothair
bowed lowly and touched her hand with his lip.

"I was sorry to have missed you yesterday. We
had gone down to Vauxe for the day, but I heard
of you from my Lord with great pleasure. We are
all of us so happy that you have entirely recovered
your health."

"I owe that to you, dearest lady," said Lothair,
"and to those under your roof. I can never forget
your goodness to me. Had it not been for you, I
should not have been here or anywhere else."

"No, no; we did our best for the moment. But
I quite agree with my Lord, now, that you stayed
too long at Rome under the circumstances. It was

a good move—that going to Sicily, and so wise of you to travel in Egypt. Men should travel."

"I have not been to Egypt," said Lothair; "I have been to the Holy Land, and am a pilgrim. I wish you would tell Miss Arundel that I shall ask her permission to present her with my crucifix, which contains the earth of the Holy Places. I should have told her this myself, if I had seen her yesterday. Is she here?"

"She is at Vauxe; she could not tear herself away from the roses."

"But she might have brought them with her as companions," said Lothair, "as you have, I apprehend, yourself."

"I will give you this in Clare's name," said Lady St. Jerome, as she selected a beautiful flower and presented it to Lothair. "It is in return for your crucifix, which I am sure she will highly esteem. I only wish it were a rose of Jericho."

Lothair started. The name brought up strange and disturbing associations: the procession in the Jesuits' Church, the lighted tapers, the consecrated children, one of whom had been supernaturally presented with the flower in question. There was an awkward silence, until Lothair, almost without intending it, expressed a hope that the Cardinal was well.

"Immersed in affairs, but I hope well," replied Lady St. Jerome. "You know what has happened? But you will see him. He will speak to you of these matters himself."

"But I should like also to hear from you."

"Well, they are scarcely yet to be spoken of," said Lady St. Jerome. "I ought not perhaps even to have alluded to the subject; but I know how deeply devoted you are to religion. We are on the eve of the greatest event of this century. When I wake in the morning, I always fancy that I have heard of it only in dreams. And many—all this room—will not believe in the possibility of its happening. They smile when the contingency is alluded to, and if I were not present they would mock. But it will happen—I am assured it will happen," exclaimed Lady St. Jerome, speaking with earnestness, though in a hushed voice. "And no human imagination can calculate or conceive what may be its effect on the destiny of the human race."

"You excite my utmost curiosity," said Lothair.

"Hush! there are listeners. But we shall soon meet again. You will come and see us, and soon. Come down to Vauxe on Saturday; the Cardinal will be there. And the place is so lovely now. I always say Vauxe at Whitsuntide, or a little later, is a scene for Shakespeare. You know you always liked Vauxe."

"More than liked it," said Lothair; "I have passed at Vauxe some of the happiest hours of my life."

CHAPTER XXXVII.

On the morning of the very Saturday on which Lothair was to pay his visit to Vauxe, riding in the park, he was joined by that polished and venerable nobleman who presides over the destinies of art in Great Britain. This distinguished person had taken rather a fancy to Lothair, and liked to talk to him about the Phœbus family; about the great artist himself, and all his theories and styles; but especially about the fascinating Madame Phœbus and the captivating Euphrosyne.

"You have not found time, I dare say," said the nobleman, "to visit the exhibition of the Royal Academy?"

"Well, I have only been here a week," said Lothair, "and have had so many things to think of, and so many persons to see."

"Naturally," said the nobleman; "but I recommend you to go. I am now about to make my fifth visit there; but it is only to a single picture, and I envy its owner."

. "Indeed!" said Lothair. "Pray tell me its subject, that I may not fail to see it."

"It is a portrait," said the nobleman; "only a portrait, some would say, as if the finest pictures in the world were not only portraits. The masterpieces of the English school are portraits, and some day

when you have leisure and inclination, and visit
Italy, you will see portraits by Titian and Raffaelle
and others, which are the masterpieces of art. Well.
the picture in question is a portrait by a young
English painter at Rome and of an English lady.
I doubt not the subject was equal to the genius of
the artist, but I do not think that the modern pencil
has produced anything equal to it, both in design
and colour and expression. You should see it, by
all means, and I have that opinion of your taste that
I do not think you will be content by seeing it once.
The real taste for fine art in this country is proved
by the crowd that always surrounds that picture;
and yet only a portrait of an English lady, a Miss
Arundel."

"A Miss Arundel?" said Lothair.

"Yes, of a Roman Catholic family; I believe a
relative of the St. Jeromes. They were at Rome
last year, when this portrait was executed."

"If you will permit me," said Lothair, "I should
like to accompany you to the Academy. I am going
out of town this afternoon, but not far, and could
manage it."

So they went together. It was the last exhibition
of the Academy in Trafalgar Square. The portrait
in question was in the large room, and hung on the
eye line; so, as the throng about it was great, it was
not easy immediately to inspect it. But one or two
R.A.s who were gliding about, and who looked upon
the noble patron of art as a sort of divinity, insensibly controlled the crowd, and secured for their

friend and his companion the opportunity which they desired.

"It is the finest thing since the portrait of the Cenci," said the noble patron.

The painter had represented Miss Arundel in her robe of a sister of mercy, but with uncovered head. A wallet was at her side, and she held a crucifix. Her beautiful eyes, full of mystic devotion, met those of the spectator with a fascinating power that kept many spell-bound. In the background of the picture was a masterly glimpse of the papal gardens and the wondrous dome.

"That must be a great woman," said the noble patron of art.

Lothair nodded assent in silence.

The crowd about the picture seemed breathless and awe-struck. There were many women, and in some eyes there were tears.

"I shall go home," said one of the spectators; "I do not wish to see anything else."

"That is religion," murmured her companion. "They may say what they like, but it would be well for us if we were all like her."

It was a short half hour by the railroad to Vauxe, and the station was close to the park gates. The sun was in its last hour when Lothair arrived, but he was captivated by the beauty of the scene, which he had never witnessed in its summer splendour. The rich foliage of the great avenues, the immense oaks that stood alone, the deer glancing in the golden light, and the quaint and stately edifice itself, so finished and so fair, with its freestone pin-

nacles and its gilded vanes glistening and sparkling
in the warm and lucid sky, contrasted with the chilly
hours when the Cardinal and himself had first strolled
together in that park, and when they tried to flatter
themselves that the morning mist clinging to the
skeleton trees was perhaps the burst of spring.

Lothair found himself again in his old rooms,
and as his valet unpacked his toilette, he fell into
one of his reveries.

"What," he thought to himself, "if life after all
be only a dream. I can scarcely realise what is
going on. It seems to me I have passed through a
year of visions. That I should be at Vauxe again!
A roof I once thought rife with my destiny. And
perhaps it may prove so. And were it not for the
memory of one event, I should be a ship without a
rudder."

There were several guests in the house, and
when Lothair entered the drawing-room, he was
glad to find that it was rather full. The Cardinal
was by the side of Lady St. Jerome when Lothair
entered, and immediately after saluting his hostess
it was his duty to address his late guardian. Lothair
had looked forward to this meeting with apprehension. It seemed impossible that it should not to a
certain degree be annoying. Nothing of the kind.
It was impossible to greet him more cordially, more
affectionately than did Cardinal Grandison.

"You have seen a great deal since we parted,"
said the Cardinal. "Nothing could be wiser than
your travelling. You remember that at Muriel I
recommended you to go to Egypt, but I thought it

better that you should see Rome first. And it answered: you made the acquaintance of its eminent men, men whose names will be soon in everybody's mouth, for before another year elapses Rome will be the cynosure of the world. Then, when the great questions come on which will decide the fate of the human race for centuries, you will feel the inestimable advantage of being master of the situation, and that you are familiar with every place and every individual. I think you were not very well at Rome; but next time you must choose your season. However, I may congratulate you on your present looks. The air of the Levant seems to have agreed with you."

Dinner was announced almost at this moment, and Lothair, who had to take out Lady Clanmorne, had no opportunity before dinner of addressing anyone else except his hostess and the Cardinal. The dinner party was large, and it took some time to reconnoitre all the guests. Lothair observed Miss Arundel, who was distant from him and on the same side of the table, but neither Monsignore Catesby nor Father Coleman were present.

Lady Clanmorne chatted agreeably. She was content to talk, and did not insist on conversational reciprocity. She was a pure freetrader in gossip. This rather suited Lothair. It pleased Lady Clanmorne to-day to dilate upon marriage and the married state, but especially on all her acquaintances, male and female, who were meditating the surrender of their liberty and about to secure the happiness of their lives.

"I suppose the wedding of the season—the wedding of weddings—will be the Duke of Brecon's," she said. "But I do not hear of any day being fixed."

"Ah!" said Lothair, "I have been abroad and am very deficient in these matters. But I was travelling with the lady's brother, and he has never yet told me that his sister was going to be married."

"There is no doubt about that," said Lady Clanmorne. "The Duchess said to a friend of mine the other day, who congratulated her, 'that there was no person in whom she should have more confidence as a son-in-law than the Duke.'"

"Most marriages turn out unhappy," said Lothair, rather morosely.

"Oh! my dear Lord, what can you mean?"

"Well I think so," he said doggedly. "Among the lower orders, if we may judge from the newspapers, they are always killing their wives, and in our class we get rid of them in a more polished way, or they get rid of us."

"You quite astonish me with such sentiments," said Lady Clanmorne. "What would Lady St. Jerome think if she heard you, who told me the other day that she believed you to be a faultless character? And the Duchess too, your friend's mamma, who thinks you so good, and that it is so fortunate for her son to have such a companion?"

"As for Lady St. Jerome, she believes in everything," said Lothair; "and it is no compliment that she believes in me. As for my friend's mamma, her ideal character, according to you, is the Duke of Brecon, and I cannot pretend to compete with him. He may please the Duchess, but I cannot say the Duke of Brecon is a sort of man I admire."

"Well, he is no great favourite of mine," said Lady Clanmorne; "I think him overbearing and selfish, and I should not like at all to be his wife."

"What do you think of Lady Corisande?" said Lothair.

"I admire her more than any girl in society, and I think she will be thrown away on the Duke of Brecon. She is clever and she has strong character, and, I am told, is capable of great affections. Her manners are good, finished and natural; and she is beloved by her young friends, which I always think a test."

"Do you think her handsome?"

"There can be no question about that: she is beautiful, and her beauty is of a high class. I admire her much more than all her sisters. She has a grander mien."

"Have you seen Miss Arundel's picture at the Academy?"

"Everybody has seen that: it has made a fury."

"I heard an eminent judge say to-day, that it was the portrait of one who must be a great woman."

"Well, Miss Arundel is a remarkable person."

"Do you admire her?"

"I have heard first-rate critics say that there was no person to be compared to Miss Arundel. And unquestionably it is a most striking countenance: that profound brow and those large deep eyes—and then her figure is so fine; but, to tell you the truth, Miss Arundel is a person I never could make out."

"I wonder she does not marry," said Lothair.

"She is very difficult," said Lady Clanmorne. "Perhaps, too, she is of your opinion about marriage."

"I have a good mind to ask her after dinner whether she is," said Lothair. "I fancy she would not marry a Protestant?"

"I am no judge of such matters," said Lady Clanmorne; "only I cannot help thinking that there would be more chance of a happy marriage when both were of the same religion."

"I wish we were all of the same religion. Do not you?"

"Well, that depends a little on what the religion might be."

"Ah!" sighed Lothair, "what between religion and marriage and some other things, it appears to me one never has a tranquil moment. I wonder what religious school the Duke of Brecon belongs to? Very high and dry, I should think."

The moment the gentlemen returned to the drawing-room Lothair singled out Miss Arundel, and attached himself to her.

"I have been to see your portrait to-day," he said. She changed colour.

"I think it," he continued, "the triumph of modern art, and I could not easily fix on any production of the old masters that excels it."

"It was painted at Rome," she said, in a low voice.

"So I understood. I regret that when I was at Rome I saw so little of its art. But my health you know was wretched. Indeed, if it had not been for some friends—I might say for one friend—I should not have been here or in this world. I can never express to that person my gratitude, and it increases every day. All that I have dreamed of angels was then realised."

"You think too kindly of us."

"Did Lady St. Jerome give you my message about the earth from the holy places which I had placed in a crucifix, and which I hope you will accept from me, in remembrance of the past and your Christian kindness to me? I should have left it at St. James's Square before this, but it required some little arrangement after its travels."

"I shall prize it most dearly, both on account of its consecrated character and for the donor's sake, whom I have ever wished to see the champion of our Master."

"You never had a wish, I am sure," said Lothair, "that was not sublime and pure."

CHAPTER XXXVIII.

THEY breakfasted at Vauxe, in the long gallery.
It was always a merry meal, and it was the fashion
of the house that all should be present. The Cardinal was seldom absent. He used to say, "I feel
more on equal terms with my friends at breakfast,
and rather look forward to my banquet of dry toast."
Lord St. Jerome was quite proud of receiving his
letters and newspapers at Vauxe earlier by far than
he did at St. James's Square; and as all were
supplied with their letters and journals, there was a
great demand for news, and a proportional circula-
tion of it. Lady Clanmorne indulged this passion
for gossip amusingly one morning, and read a letter
from her correspondent, written with the grace of a
Sévigné, but which contained details of marriages,
elopements, and a murder among their intimate acquaintance, which made all the real intelligence
quite insipid, and was credited for at least half an
hour.

The gallery at Vauxe was of great length, and
the breakfast-table was laid at one end of it. The
gallery was of panelled oak, with windows of stained
glass in the upper panes, and the ceiling, richly and
heavily carved, was entirely gilt, but with deadened
gold. Though stately, the general effect was not
free from a certain character of gloom. Lit, as it

was, by sconces, this was at night much softened; but on a rich summer morn, the gravity and repose of this noble chamber were grateful to the senses.

The breakfast was over; the ladies had retired, stealing off with the "Morning Post," the gentlemen gradually disappearing for the solace of their cigars. The Cardinal, who was conversing with Lothair, continued their conversation while walking up and down the gallery, far from the hearing of the servants, who were disembarrassing the breakfast-table, and preparing it for luncheon. A visit to a country house, as Pinto says, is a series of meals mitigated by the new dresses of the ladies.

"The more I reflect on your travels," said the Cardinal, "the more I am satisfied with what has happened. I recognise the hand of Providence in your preliminary visit to Rome and your subsequent one to Jerusalem. In the vast events which are impending, that man is in a strong position who has made a pilgrimage to the Holy Sepulchre. You remember our walk in the park here," continued the Cardinal; "I felt then that we were on the eve of some mighty change, but it was then indefinite, though to me inevitable. You were destined, I was persuaded, to witness it, even, as I hoped, to take no inconsiderable share in its fulfilment. But I hardly believed that I should have been spared for this transcendent day, and when it is consummated, I will gratefully exclaim, 'Nunc me dimittis!'"

"You allude, sir, to some important matter which Lady St. Jerome a few days ago intimated to me,

17*

but it was only an intimation, and purposely very vague."

"There is no doubt," said the Cardinal, speaking with solemnity, "of what I now communicate to you. The Holy Father, Pius IX., has resolved to summon an Œcumenical Council."

"An Œcumenical Council!" said Lothair.

"It is a weak phrase," resumed the Cardinal, "to say it will be the greatest event of this century. I believe it will be the greatest event since the Episcopate of St. Peter; greater, in its consequences to the human race, than the fall of the Roman Empire, the pseudo-Reformation, or the Revolution of France. It is much more than three hundred years since the last Œcumenical Council, the Council of Trent, and the world still vibrates with its decisions. But the Council of Trent, compared with the impending Council of the Vatican, will be as the mediæval world of Europe compared with the vast and complete globe which man has since discovered and mastered."

"Indeed!" said Lothair.

"Why the very assembly of the Fathers of the Church will astound the Freemasons, and the Secret Societies, and the Atheists. That alone will be a demonstration of power on the part of the Holy Father which no conqueror from Sesostris to Napoleon has ever equalled. It was only the bishops of Europe that assembled at Trent, and, inspired by the Holy Spirit, their decisions have governed man for more than three hundred years. But now the bishops of the whole world will assemble round the chair of

St. Peter, and prove by their presence the catholic character of the Church. Asia will send its patriarchs and pontiffs, and America and Australia its prelates; and at home, my dear young friend, the Council of the Vatican will offer a striking contrast to the Council of Trent; Great Britain will be powerfully represented. The bishops of Ireland might have been counted on, but it is England also that will send her prelates now, and some of them will take no ordinary share in transactions that will give a new form and colour to human existence."

"Is it true, sir, that the object of the Council is to declare the infallibility of the Pope?"

"In matters of faith and morals," said the Cardinal quickly. "There is no other infallibility. That is a secret with God. All that we can know of the decision of the Council on this awful head is that its decision, inspired by the Holy Spirit, must infallibly be right. We must await that decision, and, when made known, we must embrace it, not only with obedience, but with the interior assent of mind and will. But there are other results of the Council on which we may speculate; and which, I believe, it will certainly accomplish:—first, it will show in a manner that cannot be mistaken that there is only one alternative for the human intellect: Rationalism or Faith; and, secondly, it will exhibit to the Christian powers the inevitable future they are now preparing for themselves."

"I am among the faithful," said Lothair.

"Then you must be a member of the Church Catholic," said the Cardinal. "The basis on which

God has willed that His revelation should rest in the world is the testimony of the Catholic Church, which, if considered only as a human and historical witness, affords the highest and most certain evidence for the fact and the contents of the Christian religion. If this be denied, there is no such thing as history. But the Catholic Church is not only a human and historical witness of its own origin, constitution, and authority, it is also a supernatural and divine witness, which can neither fail nor err. When it œcumenically speaks, it is not merely the voice of the Fathers of the world; it declares what 'it hath seemed good to the Holy Ghost and to us.' "

There was a pause, and then Lothair remarked: —"You said, sir, that the Council would show to the civil powers of the Christian world the inevitable future they are preparing for themselves?"

"Even so. Now mark this, my child. At the Council of Trent the Christian powers were represented, and properly so. Their seats will be empty at the Council of the Vatican. What does that mean? The separation between Church and State, talked of for a long time, now demonstrated. And what does separation between Church and State mean? That society is no longer consecrated. The civil governments of the world no longer profess to be Catholic. The faithful indeed among their subjects will be represented at the Council by their pastors, but the civil powers have separated themselves from the Church; either by royal edict, or legislative enactment, or revolutionary changes, they have abolished the legal status of the Catholic Church within their territory. It is not their choice; they are urged on by an invisible power that is anti-Christian, and which is the true, natural, and implacable enemy of the one visible and universal Church. The coming anarchy is called progress, because it advances along the line of departure from the old Christian order of the world. Christendom was the offspring of the Christian family, and the foundation of the Christian family is the sacrament of matrimony, the spring of all domestic and public morals. The anti-Christian societies are opposed to the principle of home. When they have destroyed the hearth, the morality of society will perish. A settlement in the foundations may be slow in sinking, but it brings all down at last. The next step in de-Christianising the political life of nations is to establish national education without Christianity. This is systematically aimed at wherever the revolution has its way. The period and policy of Julian are returning. Some think this bodes ill for the Church; no, it is the State that will suffer. The Secret Societies are hurrying the civil governments of the world, and mostly the governments who disbelieve in their existence, to the brink of a precipice, over which monarchies and law and civil order will ultimately fall and perish together."

"Then all is hopeless," said Lothair.

"To human speculation," said the Cardinal; "but none can fathom the mysteries of Divine interposition. This coming Council may save society, and on that I would speak to you most earnestly. His

Holiness has resolved to invite the schismatic priest-
hoods to attend it and labour to bring about the
unity of Christendom. He will send an ambassador
to the Patriarch of the heresy of Photius which is
called the Greek Church. He will approach Lam-
beth. I have little hope of the latter, though there
is more than one of the Anglican bishops who revere
the memory and example of Laud. But I by no
means despair of your communion being present in
some form at the Council. There are true spirits at
Oxford who sigh for unity. They will form, I hope,
a considerable deputation; but, as not yet being prelates, they cannot take their seats formally in the
Council, I wish, in order to increase and assert their
influence, that they should be accompanied by a
band of powerful laymen, who shall represent the
pious and pure mind of England—the coming guardians of the land in the dark hour that may be at
hand. Considering your previous knowledge of
Rome, your acquaintance with its eminent men and
its language, and considering too, as I well know,
that the Holy Father looks to you as one marked
out by Providence to assert the truth, it would please
me—and, trust me, it would be wise in you—were
you to visit Rome on this sublime occasion, and perhaps put your mark on the world's history."

"It must yet be a long time before the Council
meets," said Lothair, after a pause.

"Not too long for preparation," replied the Cardinal. "From this hour, until its assembling, the
pulse of humanity will throb. Even at this hour
they are speaking of the same matters as ourselves

alike on the Euphrates and the St. Lawrence. The good Catesby is in Ireland, conferring with the bishops, and awakening them to the occasion. There is a party among them narrow-minded and local, the effects of their education. There ought not to be an Irish priest who was not brought up at the Propaganda. You know that admirable institution. We had some happy hours at Rome together—may we soon repeat them! You were very unwell there; next time you will judge of Rome in health and vigour."

CHAPTER XXXIX.

THEY say there is a skeleton in every house; it may be doubted. What is more certain are the sorrow and perplexity which sometimes, without a warning and preparation, suddenly fall upon a family living in a world of happiness and ease, and meriting their felicity by every gift of fortune and disposition.

Perhaps there never was a circle that enjoyed life more, and deserved to enjoy life more, than the Brentham family. Never was a family more admired and less envied. Nobody grudged them their happy gifts and accidents, for their demeanour was so winning, and their manners so cordial and sympathetic, that everyone felt as if he shared their amiable prosperity. And yet, at this moment, the Duchess, whose countenance was always as serene

as her soul, was walking with disturbed visage and
agitated step up and down the private room of the
Duke; while his Grace, seated, his head upon his
arm, and with his eyes on the ground, was apparently in anxious thought.

Now what had happened? It seems that these
excellent parents had become acquainted, almost at
the same moment, with two astounding and disturbing facts: their son wanted to marry Euphrosyne
Cantacuzene, and their daughter would not marry
the Duke of Brecon.

"I was so perfectly unprepared for the communication," said the Duke, looking up, "that I
have no doubt I did not express myself as I ought
to have done. But I do not think I said anything
wrong. I showed surprise, sorrow—no anger. I was
careful not to say anything to hurt his feelings—
that is a great point in these matters—nothing dis-
respectful of the young lady. I invited him to speak
to me again about it when I had a little got over
my surprise."

"It is really a catastrophe," exclaimed the
Duchess; "and only think I came to you for sympathy in my sorrow, which, after all, though distressing, is only a mortification!"

"I am very sorry about Brecon," said the Duke,
"who is a man of honour, and who would have
suited us very well; but, my dear Augusta, I never
took exactly the same view of this affair as you did
—I was never satisfied that Corisande returned his
evident, I might say avowed, admiration of her."

"She spoke of him always with great respect,"

said the Duchess, "and that is much in a girl of Corisande's disposition. I never heard her speak of any of her admirers in the same tone—certainly not of Lord Carisbrooke; I was quite prepared for her rejection of him. She never encouraged him."

"Well," said the Duke, "I grant you it is mortifying—infinitely distressing; and Brecon is the last man I could have wished that it should occur to; but, after all, our daughter must decide for herself in such affairs. She is the person most interested in the event. I never influenced her sisters in their choice, and she also must be free. The other subject is more grave."

"If we could only ascertain who she really is," said the Duchess.

"According to Bertram, fully our equal; but I confess I am no judge of Levantine nobility," his Grace added, with a mingled expression of pride and despair.

"That dreadful travelling abroad!" exclaimed the Duchess. "I always had a foreboding of something disastrous from it. Why should he have gone abroad, who has never been to Ireland, or seen half the counties of his own country?"

"They all will go," said the Duke; "and I thought, with St. Aldegonde, he was safe from getting into any scrape of this kind."

"I should like to speak to Granville about it," said the Duchess. "When he is serious, his judgment is good."

"I am to see St. Aldegonde before I speak to

Bertram," said the Duke. "I should not be surprised if he were here immediately."

One of the social mysteries is, "how things get
about!" It was not the interest of any of the persons immediately connected with the subject that
society should be aware that the Lady Corisande
had declined the proposal of the Duke of Brecon.
Society had no right even to assume that such a
proposal was either expected or contemplated. The
Duke of Brecon admired Lady Corisande, so did
many others; and many others were admired by the
Duke of Brecon. The Duchess even hoped that, as
the season was waning, it might break up, and
people go into the country or abroad, and nothing
be observed. And yet it "got about." The way
things get about is through the Hugo Bohuns. Nothing escapes their quick eyes and slow hearts.
Their mission is to peer into society, like professional astronomers ever on the watch to detect the
slightest change in the phenomena. Never embarrassed by any passion of their own, and their only
social scheming being to maintain their transcendent
position, all their life and energy are devoted to the
discovery of what is taking place around them; and
experience, combined with natural tact, invests them
with almost a supernatural skill in the detection of
social secrets. And so it happened that scarcely a
week had passed before Hugo began to sniff the air,
and then to make fine observations at balls, as to
whom certain persons danced with, or did not
dance with; and then he began the curious process
of what he called putting two and two together, and

putting two and two together proved in about a fortnight that it was all up between Lady Corisande and the Duke of Brecon.

Among others he imparted this information to Lothair, and it set Lothair a-thinking; and he went to a ball that evening solely with the purpose of making social observations like Hugo Bohun. But Lady Corisande was not there, though the Duke of Brecon was, apparently in high spirits, and waltzing more than once with Lady Grizell Falkirk. Lothair was not very fortunate in his attempts to see Bertram. He called more than once at Crecy House too, but in vain. The fact is, Bertram was naturally entirely engrossed with his own difficulties, and the Duchess, harassed and mortified, could no longer be at home in the morning.

Her Grace, however, evinced the just appreciation of character for which women are remarkable, in the confidence which she reposed in the good sense of Lord St. Aldegonde at this crisis. St. Aldegonde was the only one of his sons-in-law whom the Duke really considered and a little feared. When St. Aldegonde was serious, his influence over men was powerful. And he was serious now. St. Aldegonde, who was not conventional, had made the acquaintance of Mr. Cantacuzene immediately on his return to England, and they had become friends. He had dined in the Tyburnian palace of the descendant of the Greek Emperors more than once, and had determined to make his second son, who was only four years of age, a Greek merchant. When the Duke therefore consulted him on "the catas-

trophe," St. Aldegonde took high ground, spoke of
Euphrosyne in the way she deserved, as one equal
to an elevated social position, and deserving it. "But
if you ask me my opinion, sir," he continued, "I
do not think, except for Bertram's sake, that you
have any cause to fret yourself. The family wish
her to marry her cousin, the eldest son of the Prince
of Samos. It is an alliance of the highest, and
suits them much better than any connection with us.
Besides, Cantacuzene will give his children large fortunes, and they like the money to remain in the
family. A hundred or a hundred and fifty thousand
pounds—perhaps more—goes a great way on the
coasts of Asia Minor. You might buy up half the
Archipelago. The Cantacuzenes are coming to dine
with us next week. Bertha is delighted with them.
Mr. Cantacuzene is so kind as to say he will take
Clovis into his counting-house. I wish I could induce your Grace to come and meet him: then you
could judge for yourself. You would not be in the
least shocked were Bertram to marry the daughter
of some of our great merchants or bankers. This
is a great merchant and banker, and the descendant
of princes, and his daughter one of the most beautiful and gifted of women, and worthy to be a princess."

"There is a good deal in what St. Aldegonde
says," said the Duke afterwards to his wife. "The
affair takes rather a different aspect. It appears they
are really people of high consideration, and great
wealth too. Nobody could describe them as adventurers."

"We might gain a little time," said the Duchess. "I dislike peremptory decisions. It is a pity we have not an opportunity of seeing the young lady."

"Granville says she is the most beautiful woman he ever met, except her sister."

"That is the artist's wife?" said the Duchess.

"Yes;" said the Duke, "I believe a most distinguished man, but it rather adds to the imbroglio. Perhaps things may turn out better than they first promised. The fact is, I am more amazed than annoyed. Granville knows the father, it seems, intimately. He knows so many odd people. He wants me to meet him at dinner. What do you think about it? It is a good thing sometimes to judge for oneself. They say this Prince of Samos she is half betrothed to is attaché to the Turkish Embassy at Vienna, and is to visit England."

"My nervous system is quite shaken," said the Duchess. "I wish we could all go to Brentham. I mentioned it to Corisande this morning, and I was surprised to find that she wished to remain in town."

"Well, we will decide nothing, my dear, in a hurry. St. Aldegonde says that, if we decide in that sense, he will undertake to break off the whole affair. We may rely on that. We need consider the business only with reference to Bertram's happiness and feelings. That is an important issue no doubt, but it is a limited one. The business is not of so disagreeable a nature as it seemed. It is not an affair of a rash engagement in a discreditable quarter from which he cannot extricate himself.

There is no doubt they are thoroughly reputable people, and will sanction nothing which is not decorous and honourable. St. Aldegonde has been a comfort to me in this matter; and you will find out a great deal when you speak to him about it. Things might be worse. I wish I was as easy about the Duke of Brecon. I met him this morning and rode with him—to show there was no change in my feelings."

CHAPTER XL.

THE world goes on with its aching hearts and its smiling faces, and very often, when a year has revolved, the world finds out there was no sufficient cause for the sorrows or the smiles. There is too much unnecessary anxiety in the world, which is apt too hastily to calculate the consequences of any unforeseen event, quite forgetting that, acute as it is in observation, the world, where the future is concerned, is generally wrong. The Duchess would have liked to have buried herself in the shades of Brentham, but Lady Corisande, who deported herself as if there were no care at Crecy House except that occasioned by her brother's rash engagement, was of opinion that "Mamma would only brood over this vexation in the country," and that it would be much better not to anticipate the close of the waning season. So the Duchess and her lovely daughter

were seen everywhere where they ought to be seen,
and appeared the pictures of serenity and satisfaction.

As for Bertram's affair itself, under the mani-
pulation of St. Aldegonde it began to assume a less
anxious and more practicable aspect. The Duke
was desirous to secure his son's happiness, but
wished nothing to be done rashly. If, for example,
in a year's time or so, Bertram continued in the
same mind, his father would never be an obstacle
to his well-considered wishes. In the meantime an
opportunity might offer of making the acquaintance
of the young lady and her friends.

And in the meantime the world went on, dancing
and betting and banqueting, and making speeches,
and breaking hearts and heads, till the time arrived
when social stock is taken, the results of the campaign estimated and ascertained, and the dark
question asked, "Where do you think of going this
year?"

"We shall certainly winter at Rome," said Lady
St. Jerome to Lady Clanmorne, who was paying a
morning visit. "I wish you could induce Lord
Clanmorne to join us."

"I wish so too," said the lady, "but that is impossible. He never will give up his hunting."

"I am sure there are more foxes in the Campagna than at Vauxe," said Lady St. Jerome.

"I suppose you have heard of what they call the
double event?" said Lady Clanmorne.

"No."

"Well, it is quite true; Mr. Bohun told me last night, and he always knows everything."

"Everything!" said Lady St. Jerome; "but what is it that he knows now?"

"Both the Ladies Falkirk are to be married, and on the same day."

"But to whom?"

"Whom should you think?"

"I will not even guess," said Lady St. Jerome.

"Clare," she said to Miss Arundel, who was engaged apart, "you always find out conundrums. Lady Clanmorne has got some news for us. Lady Flora Falkirk and her sister are going to be married, and on the same day. And to whom, think you?"

"Well, I should think that somebody has made Lord Carisbrooke a happy man," said Miss Arundel.

"Very good," said Lady Clanmorne. "I think Lady Flora will make an excellent Lady Carisbrooke. He is not quite as tall as she is, but he is a man of inches. And now for Lady Grizell."

"My powers of divination are quite exhausted," said Miss Arundel.

"Well, I will not keep you in suspense," said Lady Clanmorne. "Lady Grizell is to be Duchess of Brecon."

"Duchess of Brecon!" exclaimed both Miss Arundel and Lady St. Jerome.

"I always admired the ladies," said Miss Arundel. "We met them at a country house last year, and I thought them pleasing in every way—artless and yet piquant: but I did not anticipate their fate being so soon sealed."

"And so brilliantly," added Lady St. Jerome.

"You met them at Muriel Towers," said Lady Clanmorne. "I heard of you there: a most distinguished party. There was an American lady there, was there not? a charming person, who sang, and acted, and did all sorts of things."

"Yes; there was. I believe, however, she was an Italian, married to an American."

"Have you seen much of your host at Muriel Towers?" said Lady Clanmorne.

"We see him frequently," said Lady St. Jerome.

"Ah! yes, I remember; I met him at Vauxe the other day. He is a great admirer of yours," Lady Clanmorne added, addressing Miss Arundel.

"Oh! we are friends, and have long been so," said Miss Arundel, and she left the room.

"Clare does not recognise admirers," said Lady St. Jerome gravely.

"I hope the ecclesiastical fancy is not reviving," said Lady Clanmorne. "I was half in hopes that the lord of Muriel Towers might have deprived the Church of its bride."

"That could never be," said Lady St. Jerome; "though, if it could have been, a source of happiness to Lord St. Jerome and myself would not have been wanting. We greatly regard our kinsman, but between ourselves," added Lady St. Jerome in a low voice, "it was supposed that he was attached to the American lady of whom you were speaking."

"And where is she now?"

"I have heard nothing of late. Lothair was in Italy at the same time as ourselves, and was ill there,

under our roof; so we saw a great deal of him.
Afterwards he travelled for his health, and has now
just returned from the East."

A visitor was announced, and Lady Clanmorne
retired.

Nothing happens as you expect. On his voyage
home Lothair had indulged in dreams of renewing
his intimacy at Crecy House, around whose hearth
all his sympathies were prepared to cluster. The
first shock to this romance was the news he received
of the impending union of Lady Corisande with the
Duke of Brecon. And what with this unexpected
obstacle to intimacy, and the domestic embarrass-
ments occasioned by Bertram's declaration, he had
become a stranger to a roof which had so filled his
thoughts. It seemed to him that he could not enter
the house either as the admirer of the daughter or
as the friend of her brother. She was probably engaged to another, and as Bertram's friend and fel-
low-traveller, he fancied he was looked upon by the
family as one who had in some degree contributed
to their mortification. Much of this was imaginary,
but Lothair was very sensitive, and the result was
that he ceased to call at Crecy House, and for some
time kept aloof from the Duchess and her daughter,
when he met them in general society. He was glad
to hear from Bertram and St. Aldegonde that the
position of the former was beginning to soften at
home, and that the sharpness of his announcement
was passing away. And when he had clearly ascertained that the contemplated union of Lady Corisande with the Duke was certainly not to take place,

Lothair began to reconnoitre, and try to resume his
original position. But his reception was not en-
couraging, at least not sufficiently cordial for one
who by nature was retiring and reserved. Lady
Corisande was always kind, and after some time he
danced with her again. But there were no invitations to luncheon from the Duchess; they never
asked him to dinner. His approaches were received
with courtesy, but he was not courted.

The announcement of the marriage of the Duke
of Brecon did not, apparently, in any degree dis-
tress Lady Corisande. On the contrary, she expressed much satisfaction at her two young friends
settling in life with such success and splendour.
The ambition both of Lady Flora and Lady Grizell
was that Corisande should be a bridesmaid. This
would be a rather awkward post to occupy under
the circumstances, so she embraced both, and said
that she loved them both so equally, that she would
not give a preference to either, and therefore, though
she certainly would attend their weddings, she would
refrain from taking part in the ceremony.

The Duchess went with Lady Corisande one
morning to Mr. Ruby's to choose a present from her
daughter to each of the young ladies. Mr. Ruby in
a back shop poured forth his treasures of bracelets,
and rings, and lockets. The presents must be similar
in value and in beauty, and yet there must be some
difference between them; so it was a rather long and
troublesome investigation, Mr. Ruby as usual varying
its monotony, or mitigating its wearisomeness, by

occasionally, or suddenly, exhibiting some splendid
or startling production of his art. The parure of an
Empress, the bracelets of Grand-Duchesses, a wonderful fan that was to flutter in the hands of Majesty,
had all in due course appeared, as well as the black
pearls and yellow diamonds that figure and flash on
such occasions, before eyes so favoured and so
fair.

At last—for, like a prudent general, Mr. Ruby
had always a great reserve—opening a case, he said,
"There!" and displayed a crucifix of the most
exquisite workmanship and the most precious
materials.

"I have no hesitation in saying the rarest jewel
which this century has produced. See! the figure
by Monti; a masterpiece. Every emerald in the
cross a picked stone. These corners, your Grace is
aware," said Mr. Ruby condescendingly, "contain
the earth of the holy places at Jerusalem. It has
been shown to no one but your Grace."

"It is indeed most rare and beautiful," said the
Duchess, "and most interesting too, from contain-
ing the earth of the holy places. A commission, of
course?"

"From one of our most eminent patrons," and
then he mentioned Lothair's name.

Lady Corisande looked agitated.

"Not for himself," said Mr. Ruby.

Lady Corisande seemed relieved.

"It is a present to a young lady—Miss Arundel."

Lady Corisande changed colour, and turning away, walked towards a case of works of art, which was in the centre of the shop, and appeared to be engrossed in their examination.

CHAPTER XLI.

A DAY or two after this adventure of the crucifix, Lothair met Bertram, who said to him, "By the bye, if you want to see my people before they leave town, you must call at once."

"You do not mean that," replied Lothair, much surprised. "Why, the Duchess told me, only three or four days ago, that they should not leave town until the end of the first week of August. They are going to the weddings."

"I do not know what my mother said to you, my dear fellow, but they go to Brentham the day after to-morrow, and will not return. The Duchess has been for a long time wishing this, but Corisande would stay. She thought they would only bother themselves about my affairs, and there was more distraction for them in town. But now they are going, and it is for Corisande they go. She is not well, and they have suddenly resolved to depart."

"Well, I am very sorry to hear it," said Lothair; "I shall call at Crecy House. Do you think they will see me?"

"Certain."

"And what are your plans?"

"I have none," said Bertram. "I suppose I must not leave my father alone at this moment. He has behaved well; very kindly, indeed. I have nothing to complain of. But still all is vague, and I feel somehow or other I ought to be about him."

"Have you heard from our dear friends abroad?"

"Yes," said Bertram, with a sigh, "Euphrosyne writes to me; but I believe St. Aldegonde knows more about their views and plans than I do. He and Mr. Phœbus correspond much. I wish to heaven they were here, or rather that we were with them," he added, with another sigh. "How happy we all were at Jerusalem! How I hate London! And Brentham worse. I shall have to go to a lot of agricultural dinners and all sorts of things. The Duke expects it, and I am bound now to do everything to please him. What do you think of doing?"

"I neither know nor care," said Lothair, in a tone of great despondency.

"You are a little hipped."

"Not a little. I suppose it is the excitement of the last two years that has spoiled me for ordinary life. But I find the whole thing utterly intolerable, and regret now that I did not rejoin the staff of the General. I shall never have such a chance again. It was a mistake; but one is born to blunder."

Lothair called at Crecy House. The hall-porter was not sure whether the Duchess was at home, and the groom of the chambers went to see. Lothair had never experienced this form. When the groom of the chambers came down again, he gave her Grace's compliments, but she had a headache, and was obliged to lie down, and was sorry she could not see Lothair, who went away livid.

Crecy House was only a few hundred yards from St. James's Square, and Lothair repaired to an accustomed haunt. He was not in a humour for society, and yet he required sympathy. There were some painful associations with the St. Jerome family, and yet they had many charms. And the painful associations had been greatly removed by their easy and cordial reception of him, and the charms had been renewed and increased by subsequent intercourse. After all, they were the only people who had always been kind to him. And if they had erred in a great particular, they had been animated by pure, and even sacred, motives. And had they erred? Were not his present feelings of something approaching to desolation a fresh proof that the spirit of man can alone be sustained by higher relations than merely human ones? So he knocked at the door, and Lady St. Jerome was at home. She had not a headache; there were no mysterious whisperings between hall-porters and grooms of the chamber, to ascertain whether he was one of the initiated. Whether it were London or Vauxe, the eyes of the household proved that he was ever a welcome and cherished guest.

Lady St. Jerome was alone, and rose from her writing-table to receive him. And then—for she was a lady who never lost a moment—she resumed some work, which did not interfere with their conversation. Her talking resources were so happy and inexhaustible, that it signified little that her visitor, who was

bound in that character to have something to say,
was silent and moody.

"My Lord," she continued, "has taken the
Palazzo Agostini for a term. I think we should
always pass our winters at Rome under any circumstances, but—the Cardinal has spoken to you about
the great event—if that comes off, of which, between ourselves, whatever the world may say, I believe there is no sort of doubt, we should not think
of being absent from Rome for a day during the
Council."

"Why! it may last years," said Lothair. "There
is no reason why it should not last as long as the
Council of Trent. It has in reality much more
to do."

"We do things quicker now," said Lady St.
Jerome.

"That depends on what there is to do. To
revive faith is more difficult than to create it."

"There will be no difficulty when the Church
has assembled," said Lady St. Jerome. "This sight
of the universal Fathers coming from the uttermost
ends of the earth to bear witness to the truth will
at once sweep away all the vain words and vainer
thoughts of this unhappy century. It will be what
they call a great fact, dear Lothair; and when the
Holy Spirit descends upon their decrees, my firm
belief is the whole world will rise as it were from
a trance, and kneel before the divine tomb of St.
Peter."

"Well, we shall see," said Lothair.

"The Cardinal wishes you very much to attend

the Council. He wishes you to attend it as an Anglican, representing with a few others our laity. He says it would have the very best effect for religion."

"He spoke to me."

"And you agreed to go?"

"I have not refused him. If I thought I could do any good, I am not sure I would not go," said Lothair; "but from what I have seen of the Roman Court, there is little hope of reconciling our differences. Rome is stubborn. Now, look at the difficulties they make about the marriage of a Protestant and one of their own communion. It is cruel, and I think on their part unwise."

"The sacrament of marriage is of ineffable holiness," said Lady St. Jerome.

"I do not wish to deny that," said Lothair, "but I see no reason why I should not marry a Roman Catholic if I liked, without the Roman Church interfering and entirely regulating my house and home."

"I wish you would speak to Father Coleman about this," said Lady St. Jerome.

"I have had much talk with Father Coleman about many things in my time," said Lothair, "but not about this. By the bye, have you any news of the Monsignore?"

"He is in Ireland, arranging about the Œcumenical Council. They do not understand these matters there as well as we do in England, and his Holiness, by the Cardinal's advice, has sent the Monsignore to put things right."

"All the Father Colemans in the world cannot alter the state of affairs about mixed marriages," said Lothair; "they can explain, but they cannot alter. I want change in this matter, and Rome never changes."

"It is impossible for the Church to change," said Lady St. Jerome, "because it is Truth."

"Is Miss Arundel at home?" said Lothair.

"I believe so," said Lady St. Jerome.

"I never see her now," he said discontentedly. "She never goes to balls, and she never rides. Except occasionally under this roof, she is invisible."

"Clare does not go any longer into society," said Lady St. Jerome.

"Why?"

"Well, it is a secret," said Lady St. Jerome, with some disturbance of countenance, and speaking in a lower tone; "at least, at present; and yet I can hardly on such a subject wish that there should be a secret from you—Clare is about to take the veil."

"Then I have not a friend left in the world," said Lothair, in a despairing tone.

Lady St. Jerome looked at him with an anxious glance. "Yes," she continued, "I do not wish to conceal it from you, that for a time we could have wished it otherwise—it has been, it is a trying event, for my Lord and myself—but the predisposition, which was always strong, has ended in a determination so absolute, that we recognise the Divine purpose in her decision, and we bow to it."

"I do not bow to it," said Lothair; "I think it barbarous and unwise."

"Hush! hush! dear friend."
"And does the Cardinal approve of this step?"
"Entirely."
"Then my confidence in him is entirely destroyed," said Lothair.

CHAPTER XLII

IT WAS August, and town was thinning fast. Parliament still lingered, but only for technical purposes; the political struggle of the session having terminated at the end of July. One social event was yet to be consummated—the marriages of Lothair's cousins. They were to be married on the same day, at the same time, and in the same place. Westminster Abbey was to be the scene, and as it was understood that the service was to be choral, great expectations of ecclesiastical splendour and effect were much anticipated by the fair sex. They were however doomed to disappointment, for although the day was fine, the attendance numerous and brilliant beyond precedent, Lord Culloden would have "no popery." Lord Carisbrooke, who was a ritualist, murmured, and was encouraged in his resistance by Lady Clanmorne and a party, but as the Duke of Brecon was high and dry, there was a want of united action, and Lord Culloden had his way.

After the ceremony, the world repaired to the mansion of Lord Culloden in Belgrave Square, to inspect the presents, and to partake of a dinner called a breakfast. Cousin Lothair wandered about the rooms, and had the satisfaction of seeing a bracelet with a rare and splendid sapphire which he had given to Lady Flora, and a circlet of diamond stars which he had placed on the brow of the Duchess of Brecon. The St. Aldegondes were the only members of the Brentham family who were present. St. Aldegonde had a taste for marriages and public executions, and Lady St. Aldegonde wandered about with Lothair, and pointed out to him Corisande's present to his cousins.

"I never was more disappointed than by your family leaving town so early this year," he said.

"We were quite surprised."

"I am sorry to hear your sister is indisposed."

"Corisande! she is perfectly well."

"I hope the Duchess's headache is better," said Lothair. "She could not receive me when I called to say farewell, because she had a headache."

"I never knew Mamma have a headache," said Lady St. Aldegonde.

"I suppose you will be going to Brentham?"

"Next week."

"And Bertram too?"

"I fancy that we shall be all there."

"I suppose we may consider now that the season is really over?"

"Yes; they stayed for this. I should not be surprised if everyone in these rooms had disappeared by to-morrow."

"Except myself," said Lothair.

"Do you think of going abroad again?"

"One might as well go," said Lothair, "as remain."

"I wish Granville would take me to Paris. It seems so odd not to have seen Paris. All I want is to see the new streets and dine at a café."

"Well, you have an object; that is something," said Lothair. "I have none."

"Men have always objects," said Lady St. Aldegonde. "They make business when they have none, or it makes itself. They move about, and it comes."

"I have moved about a great deal," said Lothair, "and nothing has come to me but disappointment. I think I shall take to croquet, like that curious gentleman I remember at Brentham."

"Ah! you remember everything."

"It is not easy to forget anything at Brentham," said Lothair. "It is just two years ago. That was a happy time."

"I doubt whether our re-assembling will be quite as happy this year," said Lady St. Aldegonde, in a serious tone. "This engagement of Bertram is an anxious business; I never saw Papa before really fret. And there are other things which are not without vexation—at least to Mamma."

"I do not think I am a great favourite of your Mamma," said Lothair. "She once used to be very kind to me, but she is so no longer."

"I am sure you mistake her," said Lady St. Aldegonde, but not in a tone which indicated any confidence in her remark. "Mamma is anxious about my brother, and all that."

"I believe the Duchess thinks that I am in some way or other connected with this embarrassment; but I really had nothing to do with it, though I could not refuse my testimony to the charms of the young lady, and my belief she would make Bertram a happy man."

"As for that, you know, Granville saw a great deal more of her, at least at Jerusalem, than you did, and he has said to Mamma a great deal more than you have done."

"Yes; but she thinks that had it not been for me, Bertram would never have known the Phœbus family. She could not conceal that from me, and it has poisoned her mind."

"Oh! do not use such words."

"Yes; but they are true. And your sister is prejudiced against me also."

"That I am sure she is not," said Lady St. Aldegonde quickly. "Corisande was always your friend."

"Well, they refused to see me, when we may never meet again for months, perhaps for years," said Lothair, "perhaps never."

"What shocking things you are saying, my dear Lord, to-day! Here, Lord Culloden wants you to return thanks for the bridesmaids. You must put on a merry face."

The dreary day at last arrived, and very quickly, when Lothair was the only person left in town. When there is nobody you know in London, the million that go about are only voiceless phantoms. Solitude in a city is a trance. The motion of the silent beings with whom you have no speech or sympathy, only makes the dreamlike existence more intense. It is not so in the country: the voices of nature are abundant, and from the hum of insects to the fall of the avalanche, something is always talking to you.

Lothair shrank from the streets. He could not endure the dreary glare of St. James's and the desert sheen of Pall Mall. He could mount his horse in the Park, and soon lose himself in suburban roads that he once loved. Yes! it was irresistible; and he made a visit to Belmont. The house was dismantled, and the gardens shorn of their lustre, but still it was there; very fair in the sunshine, and sanctified in his heart. He visited every room that he had frequented, and lingered in her boudoir. He did not forget the now empty pavilion, and he plucked some flowers that she once loved, and pressed them to his lips, and placed them near his heart. He felt now what it was that made him unhappy: it was the want of sympathy.

He walked through the Park to the residence of Mr. Phœbus, where he had directed his groom to meet him. His heart beat as he wandered along, and his eye was dim with tears. What characters and what scenes had he not become acquainted with since his first visit to Belmont! And even now, when they had departed, or were absent, what influence were they not exercising over his life, and the life of those most intimate with him! Had it not been for his pledge to Theodora, it was far from improbable that he would now have been a member of the

Roman Catholic Church, and all his hopes at Brentham, and his intimacy with the family on which he
had most reckoned in life for permanent friendship
and support, seemed to be marred and blighted by
the witching eyes of that mirthful Euphrosyne, whose
mocking words on the moonlit terrace at Belmont
first attracted his notice to her.   And then, by association of ideas, he thought of the General, and what
his old commander had said at their last interview,
reminding him of his fine castle, and expressing his
conviction that the lord of such a domain must have
much to do.

"I will try to do it," said Lothair, "and I will
go down to Muriel to-morrow."

CHAPTER XLIIL

LOTHAIR, who was very sensible to the charms
of nature, found at first relief in the beauties of Muriel. The season was propitious to the scene. August
is a rich and leafy month, and the glades and avenues
and stately trees of his parks and pleasaunces seemed
at the same time to soothe and gladden his perturbed
spirit. Muriel was still new to him, and there was
much to examine and explore for the first time. He
found a consolation also in the frequent remembrance
that these scenes had been known to those whom
he loved. Often in the chamber, and often in the
bower, their forms arose; sometimes their voices
lingered in his ear; a frolic laugh, or whispered
words of kindness and enjoyment. Such a place as
Muriel should always be so peopled. But that is
impossible. One cannot always have the most agreeable people in the world assembled under one's roof.
And yet the alternative should not be the loneliness
he now experienced. The analytical Lothair resolved that there was no happiness without sympathy.

The most trying time were the evenings. A man
likes to be alone in the morning. He writes his
letters and reads the newspapers, attempts to examine
his steward's accounts, and if he wants society can
gossip with his stud-groom. But a solitary evening

in the country is gloomy, however brilliant the accessories. As Mr. Phœbus was not present, Lothair violated the prime principles of a first-class Aryan education, and ventured to read a little. It is difficult to decide which is the most valuable companion to a country eremite at his nightly studies, the volume that keeps him awake or the one that sets him a-slumbering.

At the end of a week Lothair had some good sport on his moors—and this reminded him of the excellent Campian, who had received and answered his letter. The Colonel, however, held out but a faint prospect of returning at present to Europe, though, whenever he did, he promised to be the guest of Lothair. Lothair asked some of his neighbours to dinner, and he made two large parties to slaughter his grouse. They were grateful and he was popular, but "we have not an idea in common," thought Lothair, as wearied and uninterested he bade his last guest his last good-night. Then Lothair paid a visit to the Lord Lieutenant, and stayed two nights at Agramont Castle. Here he met many county notables, and "great was the company of the preachers;" but the talk was local or ecclesiastical, and after the high-spiced condiments of the conversation to which he was accustomed, the present discourse was insipid even to nausea. He sought some relief in the society of Lady Ida-Alice, but she blushed when she spoke to him, and tittered when he replied to her; and at last he found refuge in pretty Mrs. Ardenne, who concluded by asking him for his photograph.

On the morrow of his return to Muriel, the servant bringing in his letters, he seized one in the handwriting of Bertram, and discarding the rest, devoured the communication of his friend, which was eventful.

It seems that the Phœbus family had returned to England, and were at Brentham, and had been there a week. The family were delighted with them, and Euphrosyne was an especial favourite. But this was not all. It seems that Mr. Cantacuzene had been down to Brentham, and stayed, which he never did anywhere, a couple of days. And the Duke was particularly charmed with Mr. Cantacuzene. This gentleman, who was only in the earlier term of middle age, and looked younger than his age, was distinguished in appearance, highly polished, and singularly acute. He appeared to be the master of great wealth, for he offered to make upon Euphrosyne any settlement which the Duke desired. He had no son, and did not wish his sons-in-law to be sighing for his death. He wished his daughters, therefore, to enjoy the bulk of their inheritance in his lifetime. He told the Duke that he had placed one hundred thousand pounds in the names of trustees on the marriage of Madame Phœbus, to accumulate, "and when the genius and vanity of her husband are both exhausted, though I believe they are inexhaustible," remarked Mr. Cantacuzene, "it will be a nest's egg for them to fall back upon, and at least save them from penury." The Duke had no doubt that Mr. Cantacuzene was of imperial lineage. But the latter portion of the letter was the most

deeply interesting to Lothair. Bertram wrote that
his mother had just observed that she thought the
Phœbus family would like to meet Lothair, and
begged Bertram to invite him to Brentham. The
letter ended by an urgent request, that, if disengaged,
he should arrive immediately.

Mr. Phœbus highly approved of Brentham. All
was art, and art of a high character. He knew no
residence with an aspect so thoroughly. Aryan.
Though it was really a family party, the house was
quite full; at least, as Bertram said to Lothair on
his arrival, "there is only room for you—and you
are in your old quarters."

"That is exactly what I wished," said Lothair.

He had to escort the Duchess to dinner. Her
manner was of old days. "I thought you would
like to meet your friends," she said.

"It gives me much pleasure, but much more to
find myself again at Brentham."

"There seems every prospect of Bertram being
happy. We are enchanted with the young lady.
You know her, I believe, well? The Duke is highly
pleased with her father, Mr. Cantacuzene—he says
one of the most sensible men he ever met, and a
thorough gentleman, which he may well be, for I
believe there is no doubt he is of the highest descent
—emperors they say, princes even now. I wish you
could have met him, but he would only stay eight-
and-forty hours. I understand his affairs are vast."

"I have always heard a considerable person;
quite the head of the Greek community in this
country—indeed, in Europe generally."

"I see by the morning papers that Miss Arundel has taken the veil."

"I missed my papers to-day," said Lothair, a little agitated, "but I have long been aware of her intention of doing so."

"Lady St. Jerome will miss her very much. She was quite the soul of the house."

"It must be a great and painful sacrifice," said Lothair; "but, I believe, long meditated. I remember when I was at Vauxe, nearly two years ago, that I was told this was to be her fate. She was quite determined on it."

"I saw the beautiful crucifix you gave her at Mr. Ruby's."

"It was a homage to her for her great goodness to me when I was ill at Rome—and it was difficult to find anything that would please or suit her. I fixed on the crucifix, because it permitted me to transfer to it the earth of the holy places, which were included in the crucifix, that was given to me by the monks of the Holy Sepulchre, when I made my pilgrimage to Jerusalem."

In the evening St. Aldegonde insisted on their dancing, and he engaged himself to Madame Phœbus. Bertram and Euphrosyne seemed never separated; Lothair was successful in inducing Lady Corisande to be his partner.

"Do you remember your first ball at Crecy House?" asked Lothair. "You are not nervous now?"

"I would hardly say that," said Lady Corisande, "though I try not to show it."

"It was the first ball for both of us," said Lothair. "I have not danced so much in the interval as you have. Do you know, I was thinking, just now, I have danced oftener with you than with anyone else?"

"Are not you glad about Bertram's affair ending so well?"

"Very; he will be a happy man. Everybody is happy, I think, except myself."

In the course of the evening, Lady St. Aldegonde, on the arm of Lord Montairy, stopped for a moment as she passed Lothair, and said: "Do you remember our conversation at Lord Culloden's breakfast? Who was right about mamma?"

They passed their long summer days in rambling and riding, and in wondrous new games which they played in the hall. The striking feature, however, were the matches at battledore and shuttlecock between Madame Phœbus and Lord St. Aldegonde, in which the skill and energy displayed were supernatural, and led to betting. The evenings were always gay; sometimes they danced; more or less they always had some delicious singing. And Mr. Phœbus arranged some tableaux most successfully.

All this time, Lothair hung much about Lady Corisande; he was by her side in the riding parties, always very near her when they walked, and sometimes he managed unconsciously to detach her from the main party, and they almost walked alone. If he could not sit by her at dinner, he joined her immediately afterwards, and whether it were a dance, a tableau, or a new game, somehow or other he seemed always to be her companion.

It was about a week after the arrival of Lothair, and they were at breakfast at Brentham, in that bright room full of little round tables which Lothair always admired, looking, as it did, upon a garden of many colours.

"How I hate modern gardens," said St. Aldegonde. "What a horrid thing this is! One might as well have a mosaic pavement there. Give me cabbage-roses, sweet-peas, and wallflowers. That is my idea of a garden. Corisande's garden is the only sensible thing of the sort."

"One likes a mosaic pavement to look like a garden," said Euphrosyne, "but not a garden like a mosaic pavement."

"The worst of these mosaic beds," said Madame Phœbus, "is, you can never get a nosegay, and if it were not for the kitchen-garden, we should be destitute of that gayest and sweetest of creations."

"Corisande's garden is, since your first visit to Brentham," said the Duchess to Lothair. "No flowers are admitted that have not perfume. It is very old-fashioned. You must get her to show it you."

It was agreed that after breakfast they should go and see Corisande's garden. And a party did go— all the Phœbus family, and Lord and Lady St. Aldegonde, and Lady Corisande, and Bertram and Lothair.

In the pleasure-grounds of Brentham were the remains of an ancient garden of the ancient house

that had long ago been pulled down. When the
modern pleasure-grounds were planned and created,
notwithstanding the protests of the artists in landscape, the father of the present Duke would not
allow this ancient garden to be entirely destroyed,
and you came upon its quaint appearance in the
dissimilar world in which it was placed, as you
might in some festival of romantic costume upon a
person habited in the courtly dress of the last century. It was formed upon a gentle southern slope,
with turfen terraces walled in on three sides, the
fourth consisting of arches of golden yew. The
Duke had given this garden to Lady Corisande, in
order that she might practise her theory, that flower-
gardens should be sweet and luxuriant, and not hard
and scentless imitations of works of art. Here, in
their season, flourished abundantly all those pro-
ductions of nature which are now banished from our
once delighted senses: huge bushes of honey-suckle,
and bowers of sweet-pea and sweet-briar, and jes-
samine clustering over the walls, and gillyflowers
scenting with their sweet breath the ancient bricks
from which they seemed to spring. There were
banks of violets which the southern breeze always
stirred, and mignonette filled every vacant nook.
As they entered now, it seemed a blaze of roses
and carnations, though one recognised in a moment
the presence of the lily, the heliotrope, and the
stock. Some white peacocks were basking on the
southern wall, and one of them, as their visitors
entered, moved and displayed its plumage with
scornful pride. The bees were busy in the air, but

their homes were near, and you might watch them labouring in their glassy hives.

"Now, is not Corisande quite right?" said Lord St. Aldegonde, as he presented Madame Phœbus with a garland of woodbine, with which she said she would dress her head at dinner. All agreed with him, and Bertram and Euphrosyne adorned each other with carnations, and Mr. Phœbus placed a flower on the uncovered head of Lady St. Aldegonde, according to the principles of high art, and they sauntered and rambled in the sweet and sunny air amid a blaze of butterflies and the ceaseless hum of bees.

Bertram and Euphrosyne had disappeared, and the rest were lingering about the hives while Mr. Phœbus gave them a lecture on the apiary and its marvellous life. The bees understood Mr. Phœbus, at least he said so, and thus his friends had considerable advantage in this lesson in entomology. Lady Corisande and Lothair were in a distant corner of the garden, and she was explaining to him her plans; what she had done and what she meant to do.

"I wish I had a garden like this at Muriel," said Lothair.

"You could easily make one."

"If you helped me."

"I have told you all my plans," said Lady Corisande.

"Yes; but I was thinking of something else when you spoke," said Lothair.

"That is not very complimentary."

"I do not wish to be complimentary," said Lothair, "if compliments mean less than they declare. I was not thinking of your garden, but of you."

"Where can they have all gone?" said Lady Corisande, looking round. "We must find them."

"And leave this garden?" said Lothair. "And I without a flower, the only one without a flower? I am afraid that is significant of my lot."

"You shall choose a rose," said Lady Corisande.

"Nay; the charm is that it should be your choice."

But choosing the rose lost more time, and when Corisande and Lothair reached the arches of golden yew, there were no friends in sight.

"I think I hear sounds this way," said Lothair, and he led his companion farther from home.

"I see no one," said Lady Corisande, distressed, and when they had advanced a little way.

"We are sure to find them in good time," said Lothair. "Besides, I wanted to speak to you about the garden at Muriel. I wanted to induce you to go there and help me to make it. Yes," he added, after some hesitation, "on this spot—I believe on this very spot—I asked the permission of your mother two years ago to express to you my love. She thought me a boy, and she treated me as a boy. She said I knew nothing of the world, and both our characters were unformed. I know the world now. I have committed many mistakes, doubtless many follies—have formed many opinions, and have

changed many opinions, but to one I have been
constant, in one I am unchanged—and that is my
adoring love for you."

She turned pale, she stopped, then gently taking
his arm, she hid her face in his breast.

He soothed and sustained her agitated frame,
and sealed with an embrace her speechless form.
Then, with soft thoughts and softer words, clinging
to him, he induced her to resume their stroll, which
both of them now wished might assuredly be undisturbed. They had arrived at the limit of the
pleasure-grounds, and they wandered into the park
and into its most sequestered parts. All this time
Lothair spoke much, and gave her the history of
his life since he first visited her home. Lady Corisande said little, but when she was more composed,
she told him that from the first her heart had been
his, but everything seemed to go against her hopes.
Perhaps at last, to please her parents, she would
have married the Duke of Brecon, had not Lothair
returned; and what he had said to her that morning
at Crecy House had decided her resolution, whatever might be her lot, to unite it to no one else but
him. But then came the adventure of the crucifix,
and she thought all was over for her, and she quitted
town in despair.

"Let us rest here for a while," said Lothair,
"under the shade of this oak," and Lady Corisande
reclined against its mighty trunk, and Lothair threw
himself at her feet. He had a great deal still to tell
her, and among other things, the story of the pearls,
which he had wished to give to Theodora.

"She was, after all, your good genius," said
Lady Corisande.   "I always liked her."

"Well now," said Lothair, "that case has never
been opened. The year has elapsed, but I would
not open it, for I had always a wild wish that the
person who opened it should be yourself. See, here
it is."   And he gave her the case.

"We will not break the seal," said Lady Corisande.   "Let us respect it for her sake—ROMA!"
she said, examining it; and then they opened the
case.   There was the slip of paper which Theodora
at the time had placed upon the pearls, and on which
she had written some unseen words. They were
read now, and ran thus—

"THE OFFERING OF THEODORA TO
LOTHAIR'S BRIDE."

"Let me place them on you now," said Lothair.

"I will wear them as your chains," said Corisande.

The sun began to tell them that some hours had
elapsed since they quitted Brentham House. At last
a soft hand which Lothair retained, gave him a slight
pressure, and a sweet voice whispered, "Dearest, I
think we ought to return."

And they returned almost in silence.   They
rather calculated that, taking advantage of the
luncheon-hour, Corisande might escape to her room;
but they were a little too late. Luncheon was over,
and they met the Duchess and a large party on the
terrace.

"What has become of you, my good people?" said her Grace; "bells have been ringing for you in every direction. Where can you have been!"

"I have been in Corisande's garden," said Lothair, "and she has given me a rose."

THE END.